History Eye-witness

Flyers

Douglas Brown

HAMLYN

London · New York · Sydney · Toronto

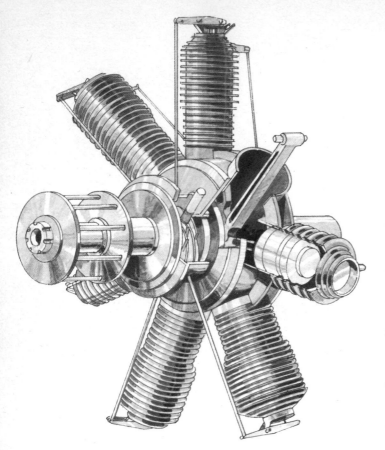

ACKNOWLEDGEMENTS

The items illustrated on the following pages are in the collections indicated:
RAF Museum, Hendon 59; Science Museum, London 12; Shuttleworth Collection, Biggleswade 18.

PHOTOGRAPHS

Aeroplane, London 50 bottom; Air France 19 bottom; Australian Information Service, London 78, 82; BBC Hulton Picture Library, London front endpapers, 15, 18 left, 35, 39, 47 left; Brisbane Airport – Dept of Transport 43 bottom, 44; British Airways 59 top; J M Bruce – Canadian Armed Forces 22 centre top left; Crown Copyright, Science Museum, London 31 top, 31 bottom; Flight International, London 55 right, 58; James Gilbert, London 32; Hamlyn Group Picture Library 34, 59 centre left, 59 centre right, 59 bottom left, 59 bottom right; John E Hoad, Milton Keynes 18 right; Imperial War Museum, London 19 top, 19 upper centre, 22 top, 22 centre top right, 22 centre bottom, 55 left, 66, 67 top, back endpapers; Lufthansa 19 lower centre; Marshall Cavendish, London – D Hoffman 12; NASA, Washington, DC 85, 88–89; RAF Museum, Hendon 22 bottom, 68; RAF Museum – Daily Mirror, London 50 centre, 50–51; Royal Aeronautical Society, London 63; Science Museum, London 47 right; Smithsonian Institution, Washington, DC 74, 75; Sport and General Press Agency, London 43 top; Michael Taylor, Cheam 19 centre, 26; Vickers 67 bottom; General Charles Yeager 72, 76, 77.

Illustrations by Derek Bunce, Mike Codd, Peter Dennis and Tony Gibbons. Maps by Bob Mathias.

First published 1981 by
The Hamlyn Publishing Group Limited
London · New York · Sydney · Toronto
Astronaut House, Feltham, Middlesex, England

ISBN 0 600 30494 9

Printed in Italy

Contents

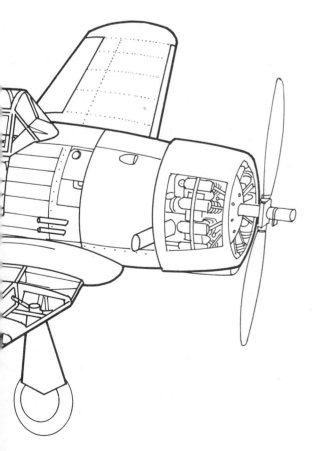

The First Flyers

Developments up to the first controlled powered flight, 1903

The opening years of the twentieth century were vital years in the story of aviation. In 1903 the brothers Orville and Wilbur Wright made the world's first controlled, powered aeroplane flight. But before then a number of determined and courageous fliers had taken to the air in a variety of flimsy experimental flying machines.

Roger Bacon was a philosopher of the thirteenth century, who first had the idea of a flying machine beating the air with its wings. Two hundred years later the artist Leonardo da Vinci designed a type of aeroplane but never built it.

In France the Montgolfier brothers made a hot air balloon. The air was heated by a fire suspended in a brazier below the balloon, and the balloon itself was made of cloth and paper.

Not surprisingly the Montgolfiers declined to travel in their creation, and the first ascent was made by Monsieur Pilâtre de Rozier, accompanied by the Marquis d'Arlandes. They took off from the Château de la Muette near Paris on 21 November 1783. During the 9-kilometre flight they had to make use of the craft's safety equipment – a wet sponge – to douse a blaze when the craft caught fire.

This successful flight inspired many balloonists. Several new designs were developed, some using hydrogen-filled balloons, and for a hundred years little progress was made with winged aircraft. Then during the 1890s a Prussian engineer named Otto Lilienthal designed and flew a series of gliders. Lilienthal's designs were similar to those of an earlier British pioneer, Sir George Cayley, who, at the start of the nineteenth century, had built several model gliders with fixed wings and a controllable tail unit. In years to come many successful aircraft designs bore a strong resemblance to Cayley's models.

The progress of flight

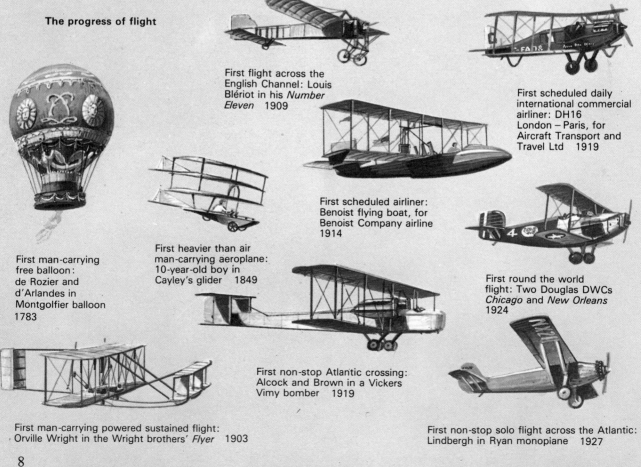

First flight across the English Channel: Louis Blériot in his *Number Eleven* 1909

First scheduled daily international commercial airliner: DH16 London – Paris, for Aircraft Transport and Travel Ltd 1919

First scheduled airliner: Benoist flying boat, for Benoist Company airline 1914

First man-carrying free balloon: de Rozier and d'Arlandes in Montgolfier balloon 1783

First heavier than air man-carrying aeroplane: 10-year-old boy in Cayley's glider 1849

First round the world flight: Two Douglas DWCs *Chicago* and *New Orleans* 1924

First non-stop Atlantic crossing: Alcock and Brown in a Vickers Vimy bomber 1919

First man-carrying powered sustained flight: Orville Wright in the Wright brothers' *Flyer* 1903

First non-stop solo flight across the Atlantic: Lindbergh in Ryan monoplane 1927

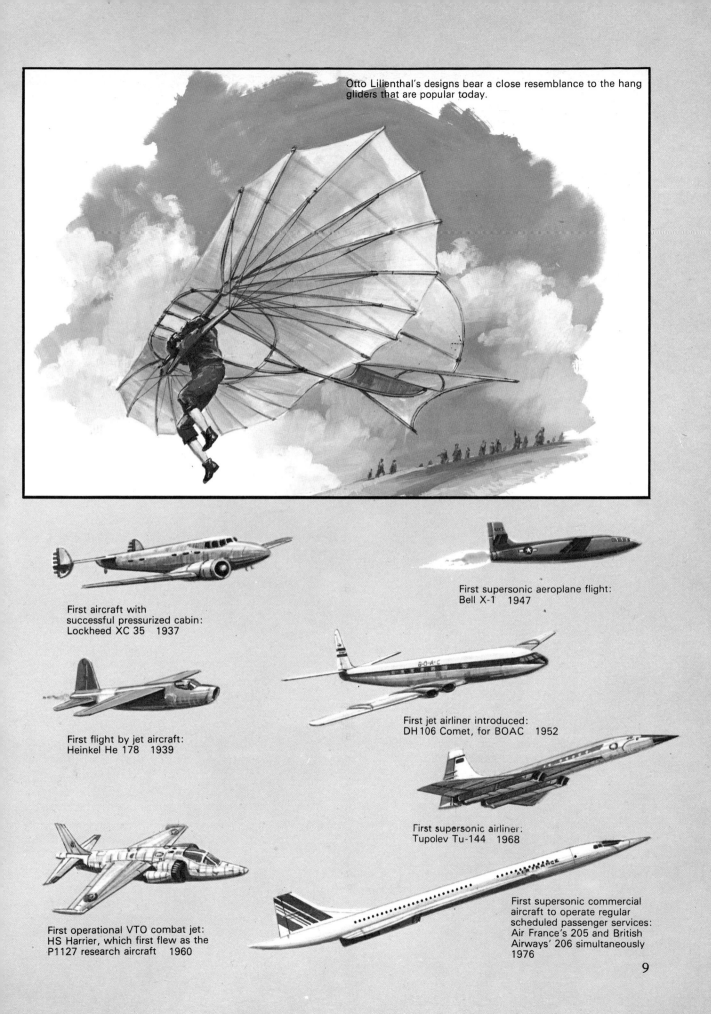

Otto Lilienthal's designs bear a close resemblance to the hang gliders that are popular today.

First aircraft with successful pressurized cabin: Lockheed XC 35   1937

First supersonic aeroplane flight: Bell X-1   1947

First flight by jet aircraft: Heinkel He 178   1939

First jet airliner introduced: DH 106 Comet, for BOAC   1952

First supersonic airliner: Tupolev Tu-144   1968

First operational VTO combat jet: HS Harrier, which first flew as the P1127 research aircraft   1960

First supersonic commercial aircraft to operate regular scheduled passenger services: Air France's 205 and British Airways' 206 simultaneously 1976

Santos-Dumont used his airship in the same way as other Parisians might have used a taxi. He thought nothing of dropping in on friends and leaving his airship tied to the house.

Lilienthal adapted Cayley's designs to make his hang gliders. He was supported in a harness beneath the glider, and by moving his body backwards and forwards and from side to side he could control the flight path. In August 1896, while trying out a moveable tail unit that he was developing, Lilienthal lost control of the glider and fell to his death. He left behind many photographs of his flights, which proved to the world that his projects were feasible, and many of the people who were designing and flying machines at that time were inspired by them.

Development of the airship

By 1900 the balloon had become a comparatively reliable means of transport, in contrast to the aeroplane which only achieved short glides and frequently crashed. During the 1880s, the German, Gottlieb Daimler, had developed the petrol engine so that it was suitable for aircraft. When the engine was fitted to a streamlined, cigar-shaped balloon, it enabled the pilot to control the path of the airship because it was no longer dependent on the wind for propulsion. However, a strong wind could still blow the airship backwards.

In 1901 Alberto Santos-Dumont, a Brazilian living in France, won a 250,000-franc prize for flying his airship *Number Six* around the Eiffel Tower in Paris. Santos-Dumont used his airship as other Parisians used their carriages, and he caused some amusement by 'dropping in' by air for a coffee at a corner café, and by his habit of

tying his balloon to a rail outside any building he was visiting. Santos-Dumont was the only airship pioneer to make his mark in fixed-wing flying as well. He produced his own aeroplane designs, but in 1910 he was crippled by illness and was an invalid for the rest of his life.

All the aeroplane designers in Europe at this time were working at building stable aeroplanes which righted themselves if upset by a gust of air. This made the craft difficult to manoeuvre as they would only fly in a straight line. In the USA at the beginning of the twentieth century, two young American brothers, Orville and Wilbur Wright, decided to design and build an unstable aeroplane. If it could be flown, they would be able to control its path through the air.

The Wright brothers were bicycle manufacturers and most of their aeronautical knowledge came from a Frenchman called Octave Chanute who lived in the USA. He had developed the designs of Otto Lilienthal into a series of advanced gliders, though he was too old to fly them himself. Although the Wrights used little from his designs, they discussed many of their own designs with Chanute and benefited from his experience.

Their first aircraft were gliders which used a system of control known as wing warping. This involved bending the wings in flight to provide roll control, and when it was combined with the Wrights' unique unstable designs it made the aircraft much more manoeuvrable than had previously been possible.

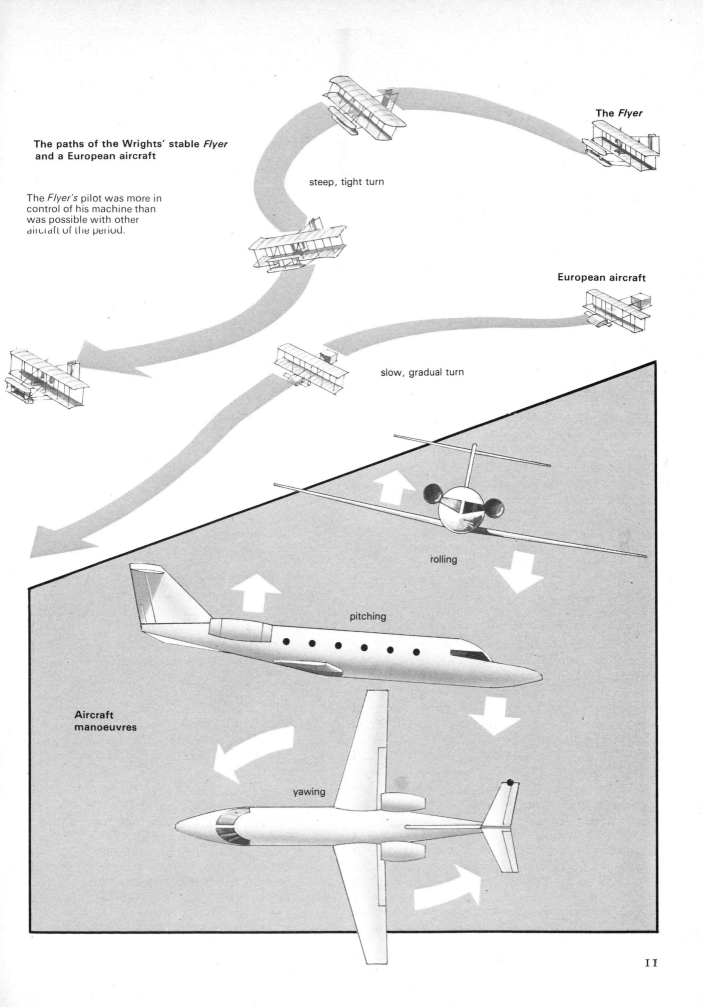

The paths of the Wrights' stable *Flyer* and a European aircraft

The *Flyer's* pilot was more in control of his machine than was possible with other aircraft of the period.

The *Flyer*

steep, tight turn

European aircraft

slow, gradual turn

rolling

pitching

Aircraft manoeuvres

yawing

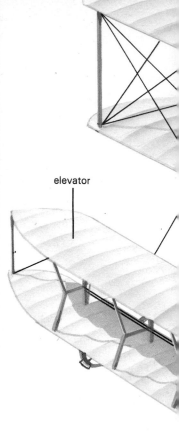

elevator

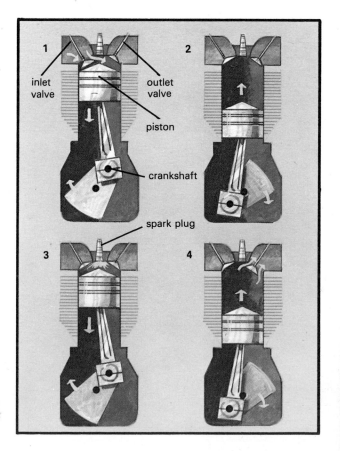

With their first three gliders the Wrights made more than 1,000 flights. Their testing ground was on the sand dunes at Kitty Hawk in the American state of North Carolina, where there were good winds for flying. By the end of 1902 both were highly experienced pilots.

Before they could try their hands at powered flight, the Wrights needed an engine, and when they could not find a suitable one they built their own. They installed it in their latest aircraft, the *Flyer*. The engine weighed 90 kilograms, one-third of the weight of the empty machine, yet it produced only 12 horsepower.

Above: The Wright brothers did not find a suitable engine, so they built their own, using a number of bicycle parts.

True mastery of the air

The *Flyer* was launched on 17 December 1903 along a rail 20 metres long at Kill Devil Sands, Kitty Hawk, with Orville Wright at the controls. The small engine, driving 2 propellers, carried the 6·5 metres long craft through the air for 12 seconds, covering just 36 metres. During the same day three more flights were made, the last with Wilbur flying. That flight covered 260 metres. The aeroplane had finally demonstrated that it could provide its pilot with true mastery of the air.

In the following years the Wrights improved their designs with more powerful engines and more manoeuvrable aircraft. Although *Flyer 3* in 1905 was travelling for 30 or 40 kilometres at speeds up to 60 kph, the Wrights could not interest any governments in their designs, and for three years they did no more flying.

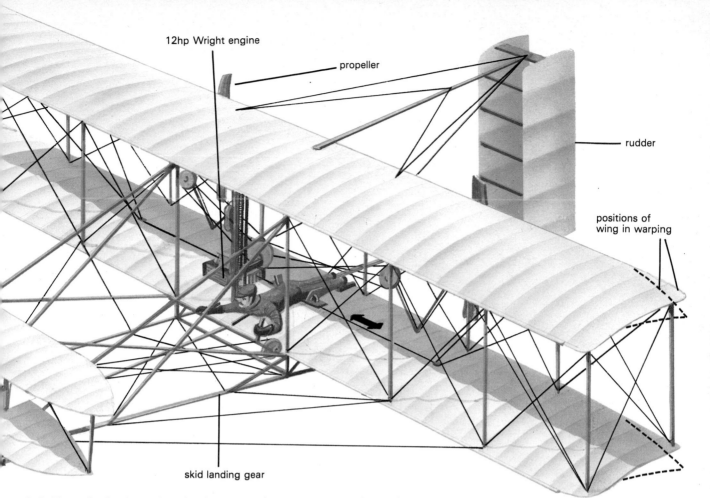

12hp Wright engine

propeller

rudder

positions of wing in warping

skid landing gear

Left: The cycle of an internal combustion engine: 1. a piston is driven down, sucking in fuel and air; 2. the piston moves up, the valves close and the fuel/air mixture is compressed in the cylinder; 3. the spark plug ignites the fuel which explodes, driving the piston down; 4. the piston moves up, driving the burnt gases out.

Above: The wing warping system, which the pilot operated by sliding from side to side, combined with the *Flyer's* lack of stability, enabled the Wright brothers to fly controlled turns and perform manoeuvres which were until then thought impossible.

Aviators in Europe were still using very stable designs which could only perform short hops in a straight line, and many people would not believe that the Wrights had progressed any further. So in 1908 the Americans were persuaded to give demonstrations in France with their aircraft modified to carry passengers. These flights were a great success and sparked off a new wave of progress in Europe, and it was twenty years before the USA regained its place in the forefront of aviation.

Below: The first flight of the *Flyer* lasted 12 seconds and covered 36 metres. The entire flight could have been made inside the 57 metre long passenger cabin of a Boeing 747, which is more than 1,000 times the weight of the Wright brothers' aeroplane.

Lufthansa

D-ABYA

13

Louis Blériot

The first flight across the English Channel, 1909

In 1901 Louis Blériot designed his first flying machine. He was a 29-year-old engineer who was having moderate success with his motor car headlight manufacturing business. Eight years later he brought to an end Britain's status as an unassailable island when he became the first man to fly across the English Channel.

His first design was an ornithopter – a machine which was meant to fly by flapping its wings. Like most designs of this type it was a failure, as were many of his later aircraft. He gradually improved their performance until, with his *Number Eight*, he achieved some success. This was really the prototype for the designs produced later by the Blériot aeroplane company. Blériot set this up to exploit his popularity after his channel crossing. Unlike the biplanes that other designers were producing which had two pairs of wings, the *Number Eight* was a monoplane with only one pair of wings. It had the engine at the front, and a horizontal tail with a rudder. In 1908 it completed a journey of 28 kilometres.

With his *Number Eleven* Blériot improved the design still further. He fitted it with Europe's first successful wing warping system for roll control and installed a three-cylinder Anzani engine of 25 horsepower.

On 13 July 1909 Blériot flew the *Number Eleven* over a 40-kilometre course to win a £200 prize offered by the French Aero Club. During the flight the engine suffered so badly from overheating that Blériot seriously burned his leg. He managed to keep the motor running until he crossed the finishing line, but for some time after the flight he could walk only on crutches. Despite this handicap he soon repaired his machine and turned his attention to another prize being offered for a course of similar length.

The English Channel

In 1908 the *Daily Mail* newspaper in London offered a prize of £500 for the first man to fly across the English Channel, and the next year they increased the award to £1,000. The first person to accept the challenge was Hubert Latham, a Frenchman of English descent, with his Antoinette monoplane. On 19 July 1909 he set out from Calais in almost perfect conditions. After only a short distance, however, the motor failed and Latham glided down to a safe landing on the water where he was quickly rescued by an escorting French warship.

Latham had the backing of Léon Levavasseur, the designer and builder of the Antoinette, and

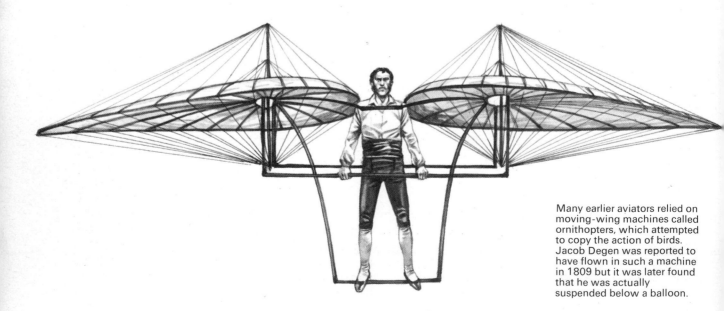

Many earlier aviators relied on moving-wing machines called ornithopters, which attempted to copy the action of birds. Jacob Degen was reported to have flown in such a machine in 1809 but it was later found that he was actually suspended below a balloon.

so a new machine was soon made available for another attempt. But before Latham could try again Blériot arrived fresh from winning the Aero Club's prize. He set up his headquarters in the village of Les Baraques, with his *Number Eleven* monoplane hurriedly repaired from the damage sustained in the previous competition. There was a third competitor, the wealthy Comte de Lambert, who established his base in Boulogne. He had bought two brand new Wright biplanes, but he was a very inexperienced pilot, and while testing one of the aircraft he crashed. Although he was not hurt he realized how foolish he would be to take part in the event with so little experience. So he withdrew from the competition and returned to Paris.

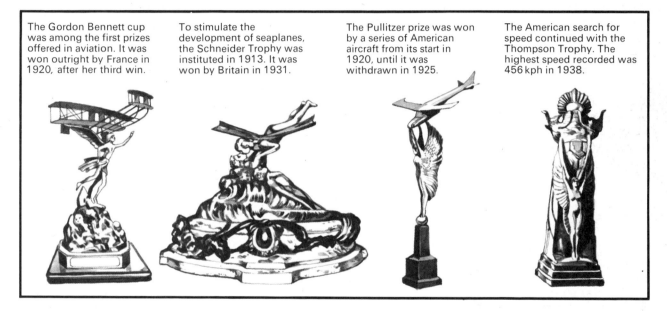

The Gordon Bennett cup was among the first prizes offered in aviation. It was won outright by France in 1920, after her third win.

To stimulate the development of seaplanes, the Schneider Trophy was instituted in 1913. It was won by Britain in 1931.

The Pullitzer prize was won by a series of American aircraft from its start in 1920, until it was withdrawn in 1925.

The American search for speed continued with the Thompson Trophy. The highest speed recorded was 456 kph in 1938.

Blériot and Latham were both ready but were delayed by bad weather. Early on 24 July one of Blériot's partners, Alfred le Blanc, woke him with the news that the weather was improving. By 4 am the tiny monoplane was ready to fly. Blériot, showing a caution that was not always so evident, first made a 15-minute test flight over Calais. Satisfied that all was well he landed near the cliffs on the French coast and at 4.35 am he took off once more, narrowly clearing some telegraph wires, and headed out over the 35-kilometre stretch of water.

Blériot had taken few special precautions for this flight. He wore the standard flyer's clothing of the period, a leather jacket, a scarf, a cap and goggles. He also wore a boilersuit which kept him reasonably warm, despite the draughts which blew through the cockpit, and gave some protection from the shower of castor oil which streamed back from the engine. Many engines at that time were lubricated with castor oil, using a 'total loss' system. This meant that the oil passed through the engine then was ejected overboard, giving the pilot a shower bath in the process. Many old aircraft still have a distinct aroma of castor oil, as at that time did most of their pilots.

Blériot had fitted a cylindrical flotation bag behind his seat to keep the aircraft afloat should he be forced to land in the sea, but he did not carry a life jacket as he expected to be rescued quickly, as Latham had been. The French navy had provided the destroyer *Escopette* as a rescue ship and guide, but the monoplane, with its tiny engine running at its maximum 1,200 rpm, flew at about 65 kph. Blériot quickly overtook the warship, so it would have been slow to rescue him, had he needed it to.

Poor visibility

By this stage Blériot was flying at a height of about 75 metres in poor visibility. Within a few minutes the French coast and the *Escopette* had disappeared into the early morning haze, and as he could not yet see the English coast Blériot had no indication of direction. There was no compass fitted to the aeroplane and the only instrument of any kind was an oil tank pressure gauge. This was essential as the pilot had to maintain the correct pressure by frequent use of a hand pump in the cockpit, or the oil would cease to flow through the engine. At the same time, the pilot had to fly the aeroplane and navigate.

As he had no compass and the sun was obscured by the mist, Blériot simply relaxed at the controls and allowed the aircraft to find its own way. He might have been more concerned if he had known that weather conditions had prevented Latham from taking off in pursuit. However, some instinct kept Blériot from straying too far from the planned course. When he eventually sighted the English coast he was close to Deal, some distance to the east of his planned landing site at Dover. Although prudence suggested an immediate landing Blériot knew that his friends were waiting for him at Dover, so he turned left and flew along the coast.

Left: Specialized flying clothes were unknown, so Blériot wore the warmest clothes available underneath a boilersuit.

Blériot's 37 minute cross-Channel flight created so much interest in his aircraft that he soon had orders for 100 of his Blériot XI model. The site of Blériot's landing, near Dover, is marked by a stone monument set into the hillside, showing the silhouette of the *Number Eleven*.

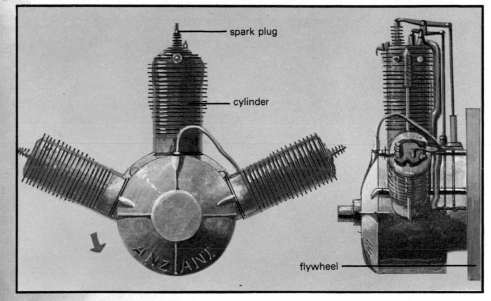

Right: The Anzani engine, which powered all the earlier Blériot monoplanes, was a fan shaped radial engine known for its unreliability. Blériot replaced the Anzani with a more powerful Gnome rotary engine in later aircraft.

spark plug

cylinder

flywheel

The Anzani engine was a constant source of trouble as it was very low-powered and unreliable. As on previous flights Blériot found that the engine was overheating and he nursed it along very carefully. Some people said that only a lucky shower of rain, which cooled the motor, prevented it from stopping completely but Blériot would never admit this. When he reached Dover he was flying quite low and was troubled by the wind around the cliffs. Just below the castle he found a gap in the cliffs and flew through it to make his landing on the Northfall Meadow.

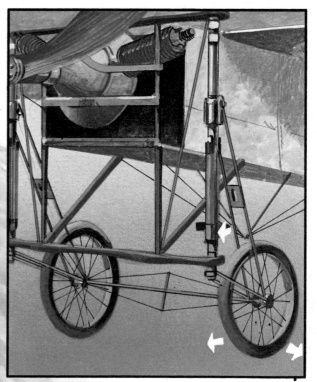

Right: The undercarriage design of Blériot's *Number Eleven* was unique, and allowed all three wheels to caster and so point in a different direction from the aeroplane.

Welcomed as a hero

The landing was the most difficult part of the flight as the main wheels of the monoplane were designed to caster. This meant that the wheels could swivel freely, so if there was any wind, or a slope on the ground, the machine could move off in a totally different direction from the one its pilot had intended. The landing at Dover presented Blériot with problems of both wind and slope. True to form, Blériot arrived in spectacular fashion, fortunately without doing any major damage either to himself or to the aeroplane. A policeman was the first person to greet the aviator after his historic flight, and shortly after him Blériot's friends arrived complete with a French flag. The large crowd which had gathered finally attracted the attention of a customs officer who was fully equipped with all the forms for clearing a ship. No one had thought of drawing up forms to clear an arriving aeroplane.

Once the formalities were over Blériot and his aircraft were taken to London. He received his prize and was welcomed as a hero, while his monoplane was displayed in Selfridges, the London store, where 120,000 people came to see it.

Far more valuable to the airman than the £1,000 prize were the orders for his aeroplanes which the successful crossing generated. However, following his experiences with the Anzani engine his later models were fitted with a Gnome engine.

Helped by the publicity created by his cross-Channel trip, Blériot's company became stronger and stronger. In 1913 he took over the SPAD company which had gone bankrupt. Blériot retained the SPAD name, and he produced the famous First World War SPAD fighters. In 1929, to celebrate the twentieth anniversary of his

Below: When Blériot landed at Dover he was met by a large crowd of wellwishers and friends who had sailed over from France.

Right: The cockpit of the Blériot *Number Eleven* was dominated by the control column topped by a wheel which was only a handgrip.

Opposite: Blériot took over the bankrupt SPAD works after SPAD's founder, Deperdussin, was imprisoned for embezzlement. Under Louis Béchéreau, the designer, several brilliant fighters were produced.
1. The S XII of 1917 which equipped many of the new American squadrons in France, and 2. the S VII of 1916.
   3. The Blériot 127 was built in the 1920s and carried four machine guns and 1,000 kilograms of bombs. In 1929 Blériot celebrated the twentieth

DOVER

Folkestone

ENGLISH CHANNEL

CALAIS

Les Baraques

BLERIOT'S FLIGHT ACROSS THE CHANNEL

crossing, Blériot again flew the Channel in one of his own aeroplanes, this time a much larger, twin-engined Blériot 127 bomber.

Blériot died in 1936, and the following year the name of his company was lost when the French aircraft industry was nationalized. Blériot's company became part of the company later known as Sud Aviation, and now called Aérospatiale. The tiny *Number Eleven* cross-Channel aeroplane which now hangs in a Paris museum was a worthy forerunner of the Concorde and Airbus Industric A300 which are now produced by Aérospatiale.

anniversary of his crossing by flying the Channel again in one of these machines.

After Blériot's death his company was nationalized, and after reorganization became part of Aerospatiale. Among the products of this descendant of the Blériot company are 4. the European A300 Airbus and 5. the Anglo-French Concorde.

Hermann Bocker

A German pilot in the First World War, 1916–1918

Early in 1916 Leutnant Hermann Bocker arrived at his first unit with the German air force, a squadron flying two-seater Roland C.11 reconnaissance aircraft. After spending six months with the army in the trenches he had volunteered for the air service, seeking a way to escape the squalid combat of the front line.

Bocker had trained on an aged Albatros aircraft and when he took off on his first combat mission he spent most of his time learning about the Roland. For this first trip his squadron commander flew with him in another Roland, and the new recruit was under strict orders not to cross the front line. He could see it away to the west marked by the smoke bursts of the anti-aircraft guns. With all his attention devoted to controlling the new aeroplane he had little time to spare for a continual surveillance of the skies. Searching for enemy aircraft was a habit which came only with experience. So when the observer, his colleague in the aircraft, tapped his shoulder and pointed towards the sun, Bocker was shocked to see an aircraft diving towards him. Fortunately, the enemy who he could now see was a Frenchman in a Nieuport, opened fire too early and then overshot his intended victim.

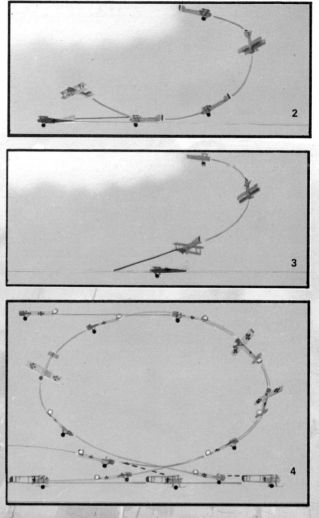

Above: Although Britain's Albert Ball preferred to attack from underneath (1) most pilots relied on height and cloud cover for surprise (2). Attacks from one side (3), were more difficult as allowance had to be made for the target's speed. The Immelmann turn (4), was used to gain a better position when being chased (green) or to continue an attack (buff).

The first lesson Bocker learned was to keep a sharp lookout for enemy aircraft, who normally attacked from out of the sun. Many inexperienced airmen were taken by surprise and shot down without ever seeing the attacking aircraft.

The commander in the other Roland waved Bocker back to base and dived towards the ground 600 metres below. Imagining that the aircraft was fleeing, the inexperienced Frenchman dived after it, putting himself in the ideal position for the German gunner to open fire with his rear firing machine-gun. As Bocker watched, pieces started to fall from the Nieuport, then smoke appeared from the engine. Within seconds the French aircraft was plunging earthwards, trailing smoke. On his return to base Bocker was overjoyed that an enemy aircraft had been destroyed on his first mission, though he had contributed little to its destruction. However, his enthusiasm was cooled by a sharp lecture from his commander on the vital necessity of keeping a constant and vigilant watch.

21

Top: The British aircraft, the Airco DH.2. Left: Cockpit of a DH.2 with instrument panel removed to show the mounting of the Lewis Gun. Above: Another British aircraft, the Vickers FB.5 Gunbus. Below left and Bottom: The German aircraft, the Albatros D.111, and its cockpit.

Bocker heeded the warning, and during the hectic air battles over the trenches, part of the great offensives of 1916, he rapidly gained experience. With experience came a very carefree lifestyle. The life expectancy of a pilot was little more than a month. During air combat the men lived mostly on their nerves, so during the evenings there were riotous parties in the mess hall. The hall was decorated with trophies taken from aircraft the squadron had shot down. The propeller of Bocker's first kill, a Vickers FB.5 Gunbus of the British Royal Flying Corps (RFC), was there. It had virtually flown across his observer's gunsight during one patrol quite close to the airfield. After landing, the two Germans had driven to the crash site and met the British pilot, who had survived the crash. As was the custom, Bocker had invited him to the mess for a celebration before sending him to captivity.

By the end of 1916 chivalrous gestures such as this were becoming less common as the war in the air intensified. Bocker was promoted to Flight Commander and though he had been flying for just six months, he was, by the standards of the day, a very experienced pilot. It was said in the air service that if a man survived for three months then he had a good chance of staying

Throughout the First World War, aircraft of both sides were powered by rotary and inline engines, although the Germans favoured the inline type. Many British and French fighters were powered by the Gnome rotary engine which was lighter than the German engines, but created more drag which affected aircraft handling.

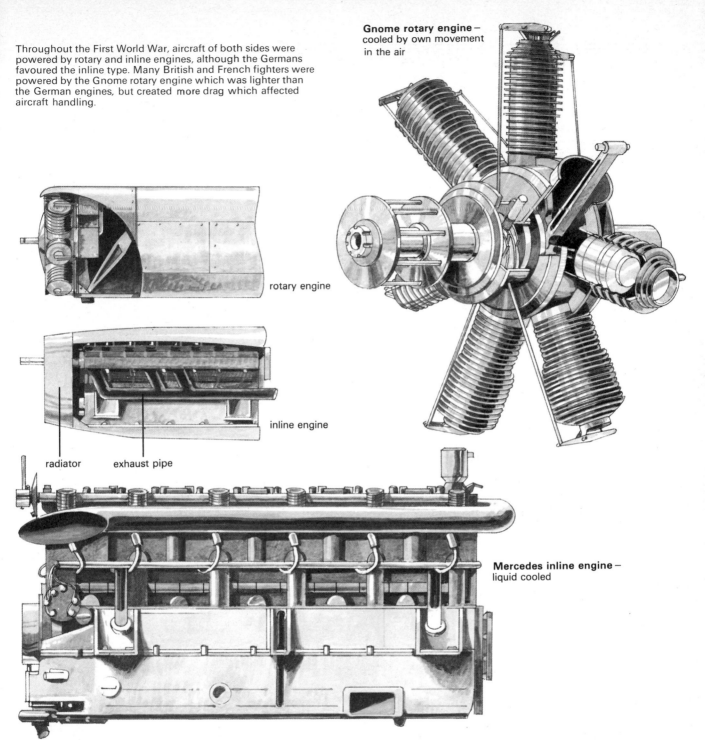

Gnome rotary engine –
cooled by own movement in the air

rotary engine

inline engine

radiator   exhaust pipe

Mercedes inline engine –
liquid cooled

alive much longer, but those first three months were critical. Bocker saw many young officers shot down within days of joining the flight, and they died because of lack of experience.

A new fighter squadron
At the end of the year the squadron was withdrawn from the front line to re-equip with the new Halberstadt ground attack aircraft. Bocker had had enough of attacking the trenches in his army days and he requested a transfer to one of the new fighter squadrons. To his delight, he was posted to the elite *Jagdstaffel Number 11*, which had recently been taken over by its new commanding officer, Baron Manfred von Richthofen. Richthofen was a popular hero, the last survivor of a great trio of fighter aces. The other two, Max Immelmann and Oswald Boelcke, had both lost their lives during 1916. Strangely, neither was shot down. Boelcke died after an aerial collision with one of his own men and Immelmann was killed when his Fokker broke up in mid-air.

Jagdstaffel 11 flew the Albatros D.III single-seaters, which were new aircraft, superior to the British and French machines. Bocker soon proved himself a competent pilot on the aircraft but he knew that his ability could not be compared with the skills of Richthofen, who had also been transferred from the army, and been promoted from the two-seater squadrons. By mid 1917 Richthofen had scored 50 victories, including one, widely reported back in Berlin, over the RFC ace Major Lanoe Hawker. After that triumph Richthofen had the machine-gun from Hawker's DH.2 fighter sent to his home to join his many other trophies. Bocker knew that in addition to the collection of mementos taken from shot-down aeroplanes, the Baron had a standing order with a local silversmith for a small cup to be made for every plane he shot down.

From Richthofen, Bocker and the other squadron pilots picked up some of the finer points of aerial combat. The British and French fighters were powered by rotary engines, which meant that while they could turn quickly in one direction, the rotation of the engine reduced the turn rate of the aircraft in the opposite direction. This made them vulnerable to the attacks of German fighters powered by in-line engines which did not affect the turn capability. At the same time the Germans formed their squadrons into circuses or *Jagdgeschwader*. Bocker frequently found himself flying in formations of fifty or sixty aircraft seeking enemy flights which also flew in large numbers. When such large numbers of aircraft joined in battle the sky was filled with whirling machines and Bocker was usually more worried by the chance of a collision than of being shot down.

A blow to the *Jagdgeschwader*

In late 1917 the squadron were flying the Fokker Dr.1 known as a triplane. On his first encounter with this aircraft Bocker was most excited by its handling qualities. It was only 6 metres long, but it carried 2 machine-guns and had a wing span of just 7 metres. This was 5 metres shorter than the Bristol fighter used by the British. Such a short wing span was possible because the craft had three wings. This made the Dr.1 a very manoeuvrable aeroplane and one that could climb quickly. Bocker soon found he could turn tighter than the Sopwith Camels of the RFC, but there was a tendency for the wings to fall off at high speed. The aircraft might soon have faded to obscurity had it not been the aircraft in which the greatest German ace, Baron von Richthofen, met his end.

The life expectancy of pilots in the First World War was short, so they lived their lives to the full, with rowdy parties in the mess most evenings.

24

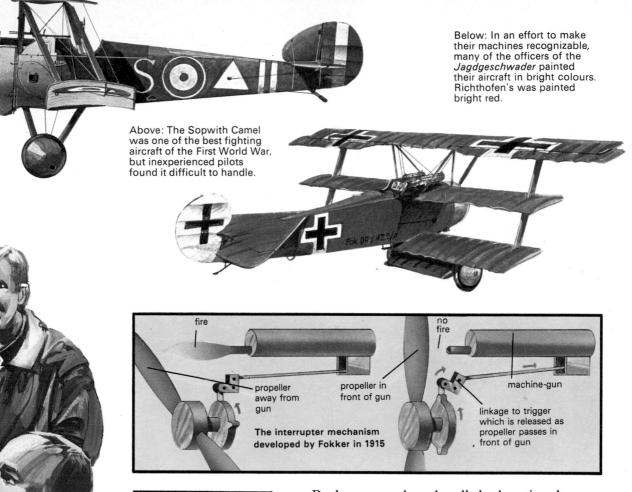

Above: The Sopwith Camel was one of the best fighting aircraft of the First World War, but inexperienced pilots found it difficult to handle.

Below: In an effort to make their machines recognizable, many of the officers of the *Jagdgeschwader* painted their aircraft in bright colours. Richthofen's was painted bright red.

fire

no fire

propeller away from gun

propeller in front of gun

machine-gun

linkage to trigger which is released as propeller passes in front of gun

The interrupter mechanism developed by Fokker in 1915

German war medals

The Iron Cross

The Blue Max

Bocker remembered well the last time he saw his commander. There had been a party in the mess the previous night to celebrate Richthofen's eightieth kill, though since he had been wounded in the head in July 1917 the Baron had not been his usual self. The next day, 21 April 1918, a patrol of Dr.1s commanded by Richthofen encountered a formation of British Sopwith Camels. Bocker saw his commander in the bright red triplane dive away in pursuit of a fleeing British aircraft. The Baron never returned to base. Later in the week a message was dropped on the German airfield by a British aircraft, to say that Manfred von Richthofen had been shot down and killed by Captain Roy Brown and buried with full military honours.

After such a blow the *Jagdgeschwader* took some time to recover. Before the new commanding officer, Hermann Goering, took over, Bocker was posted back to Berlin in a training role. This move probably saved his life, for he had already survived much longer than most pilots, and, with the development of long-range bombing of civilian and military targets, flying had caught up with the age of terrifying warfare that Bocker had left the trenches to avoid.

Alcock and Brown

The first non-stop flight across the Atlantic Ocean, 1919

The Atlantic Ocean has for centuries fascinated men seeking a challenge. The early steamships vied to reduce the crossing times. Men have sailed, rowed and ballooned over the thousands of kilometres of water. But none of these men have caught the public imagination in quite the same way as those who first attempted to fly non-stop across the North Atlantic. Many young men set out in pursuit of lasting fame, a possible knighthood and a £10,000 prize offered by Lord Northcliffe, the owner of London's *Daily Mail* newspaper.

Captain John Alcock, an Englishman, and Lieutenant Arthur Whitten Brown who was born in the USA but later took British citizenship, arrived in Newfoundland on 13 May 1919.

The Vimy was carried to America in crates and reassembled in a field in Newfoundland.

On their sea journey from England they brought, in crates, their Vickers Vimy aircraft and its two Rolls-Royce Eagle engines of 360 horsepower each.

This corner of Newfoundland is the part of North America closest to Europe, and most of the few flat areas were already occupied by other teams making their preparations for an Atlantic crossing. By early June, Alcock and Brown had found a field to use for take-off, assembled the aircraft, and were awaiting only a suitable weather report.

Weather observation in the Atlantic was primitive and relied mainly on reports by ocean liners in mid-Atlantic. Alcock and Brown knew nothing of the conditions they might encounter several thousand metres up. The forecast for 14 June was good, and so the Vimy was made ready.

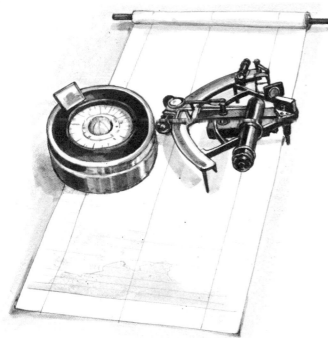

Below: The sextant and compass used by Brown for navigation, were the same as those used on board ship and were not designed for the cramped cockpit of the Vimy, 3,000 metres above the Atlantic.

Right: The morse key, named after Samuel Morse, was used to transmit the dots and dashes which make up the morse code.

Morse Code					
A	·—	M	——	Y	—·——
B	—···	N	—·	Z	——··
C	—·—·	O	———	1	·————
D	—··	P	·——·	2	··———
E	·	Q	——·—	3	···——
F	··—·	R	·—·	4	····—
G	——·	S	···	5	·····
H	····	T	—	6	—····
I	··	U	··—	7	——···
J	·———	V	···—	8	———··
K	—·—	W	·——	9	————·
L	·—··	X	—··—	0	—————
Distress signal (SOS)	···———···				
Attention signal	—·—·—				
Break	—···—				
Understood	···—·				
Received	·—·				
Position report	—·—·				
End of message	·—·—·				
Finish of transmission	···—·—				

The start of a risky journey

The take-off was the most dangerous part of a risky journey. The Vimy, a converted bomber, was laden with almost 4,500 litres of fuel. This was more than they expected to use, but it provided a reserve for any unforeseen problems. However, this extra-large fuel load increased the risk of fire in the event of a crash.

As Alcock ran the two engines up to full power, the 400 metres of cleared field ahead seemed even shorter. The aircraft accelerated slowly and was pounded by the holes and bumps in the rough field. Then, with the stone dyke marking the end of the runway looming frighteningly close, Alcock pulled the nose up and the Vimy skimmed over the wall and into the air.

The laden Vickers climbed slowly and Alcock turned inland in order to gain height before crossing the high ground near the coast. So it was some time before they crossed the coast at St John's and pointed the nose out into the vast reaches of the Atlantic.

Brown transmitted their position to the Mount Pearl radio station, but soon afterwards he realized that the morse key of his wireless telegraph, a relatively new piece of radio equipment, was not generating any signal. From then on they were out of radio contact with the ground.

While Alcock nursed the aircraft along very carefully Brown occupied himself with the navigation. The Vimy's position was checked by the same methods that ships' captains had used for the previous hundred years, by sighting the sun, moon or stars with a sextant and referring to tables, which, used in conjunction with an accurate measurement of time, gave a position in latitude and longitude which was then plotted on a chart. This operation could be difficult enough in the chartroom of a ship travelling at about 28 kph on a calm sea, but in the cramped cockpit of the Vimy, at 185 kph, while being buffeted by turbulent air currents, the margin for error was great. All of Brown's skill as a navigator was required to keep them on an accurate track.

A deafening noise

The Vimy flew on into the late afternoon. They had been flying in cloud for three hours with no chance to check their position. Alcock eased the aircraft up in an attempt to get above the cloud, but as he did so both men were terrified by a loud clattering from the starboard engine. It was with relief that they realized that it was only the exhaust pipe which, under the strain, had melted away. The resulting noise, however, was a problem, as both men were deafened and had to write notes to each other instead of merely shouting.

At last, just as the sun was setting, Brown managed to use a sextant through a gap in the clouds and confirmed that they were on course.

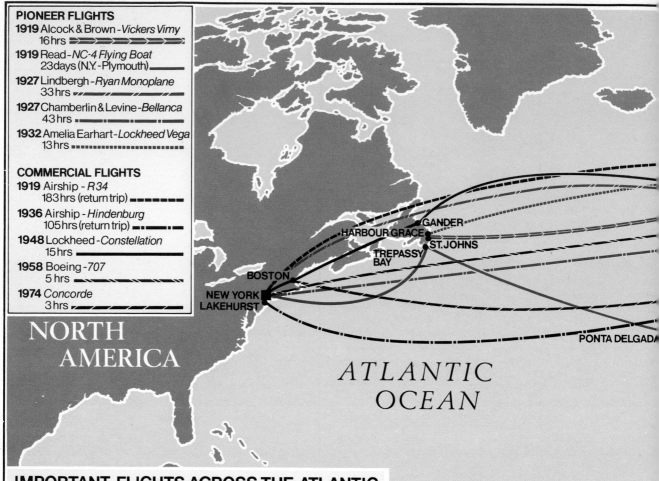

GANDER
HARBOUR GRACE
ST.JOHNS
TREPASSY BAY
BOSTON
NEW YORK
LAKEHURST
PONTA DELGADA

NORTH AMERICA

ATLANTIC OCEAN

IMPORTANT FLIGHTS ACROSS THE ATLANTIC

As darkness fell they felt very tired. The deafening engine noise and the bitter cold combined in a vicious assault on the men's senses. They wore experimental electrically heated suits which were powered by batteries, but soon after take-off the batteries went flat and the bitter cold chilled the men through. There was little thought of turning back as they knew that the other competitors waiting in Newfoundland were only too willing to take their place. Already an American, Lieutenant Commander A. C. Read, had flown the Atlantic, stopping once in the Azores, but the biggest prize – the first non-stop crossing – was theirs if they could survive a few hours more.

They were now flying in even worse conditions. Brown had made one sighting of the moon with a sextant and calculated that they had passed the halfway position, but in the early hours of Sunday morning they flew into one of the vast storm systems which dominate the North Atlantic. The aircraft was not powerful enough to fly over it, and did not have enough fuel to fly round it, so they had to go through the storm.

As the aircraft was tossed around, Alcock struggled to maintain control. His primitive flight instruments were useless, and he could not see the horizon outside, so he was fighting a losing battle. Because of the build-up of ice the airspeed indicator jammed, misleading Alcock to such an extent that he did not realize that speed was reducing. The aircraft stalled, and entered a deep spiral dive.

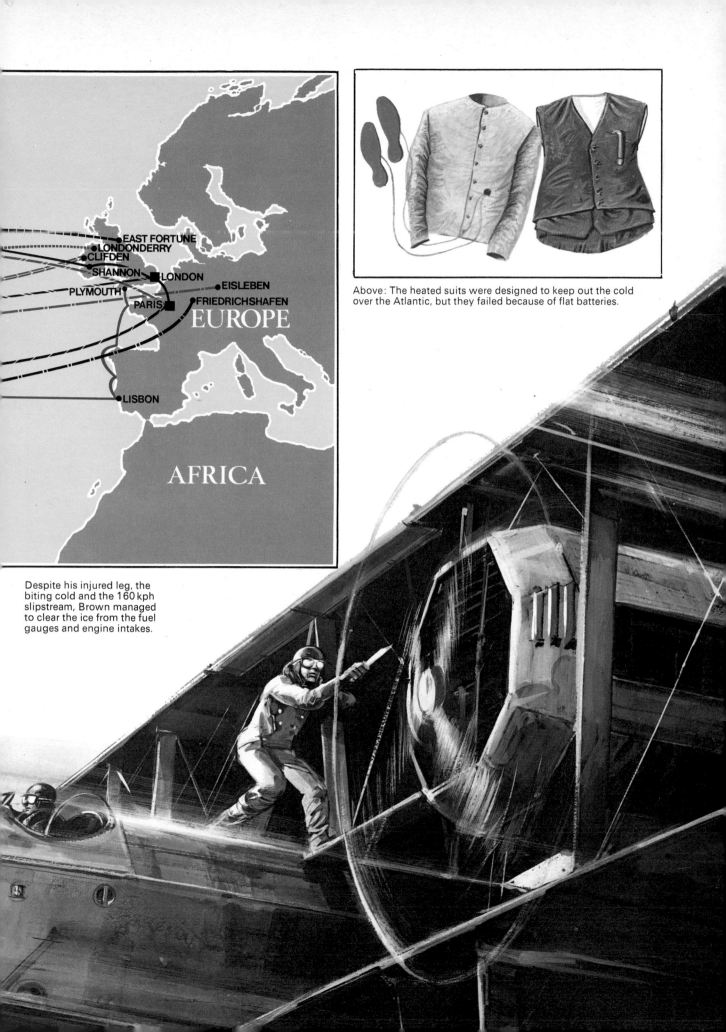

EAST FORTUNE
LONDONDERRY
CLIFDEN
SHANNON
LONDON
PLYMOUTH
PARIS
EISLEBEN
FRIEDRICHSHAFEN

EUROPE

LISBON

AFRICA

Above: The heated suits were designed to keep out the cold over the Atlantic, but they failed because of flat batteries.

Despite his injured leg, the biting cold and the 160 kph slipstream, Brown managed to clear the ice from the fuel gauges and engine intakes.

His balance was totally disturbed by the violence of the aircraft's manoeuvres, and although he was an experienced pilot, Alcock was helpless as the altimeter reading reduced rapidly. The aircraft tumbled down until it emerged from the clouds only a hundred metres above the storm-tossed seas. Alcock opened the throttles wide and struggled to bring the bomber under control as they knew that they would have little chance of surviving if they crashed into the sea. Two earlier pioneers, Hawker and McKenzie-Grieves, had floated on calm seas in their Sopwith until a passing steamer had picked them up, but Alcock and Brown's Vimy would have been smashed to pieces in the mountainous waves.

Slowly the Vimy picked up flying speed and Alcock eased the nose up towards the horizon which was now visible below the base of the cloud. With the wheels practically skimming the wave tops they began to climb away from the immediate danger. But there was further danger facing them as they gained height. Ice began to accumulate all over the aircraft. The controls became very heavy and sluggish, and Alcock was fully occupied with flying the aeroplane when both engines began to misfire. The air intakes were iced up, so reducing the power available from the engines, and handicapping the ice-laden Vimy still further.

At this point Brown, who had a crippled leg and normally walked with the aid of a stick, scrambled from the cockpit into the screaming slipstream and, clinging to the struts, he slowly chipped away the ice with his knife. First he cleared the fuel-flow gauge on the side of the engine and then, very close to the huge four-bladed propeller, he cleared the intakes themselves. Almost at once the engine picked up and Brown, already exhausted, struggled across the wing to the other engine and repeated the operation. Still the engine intakes gave trouble with ice accumulation, and several more times Brown had to repeat his courageous performance.

Because of the ice, Alcock eased the aircraft down through the clouds towards the Irish coast and towards the warmer air below. The engines were still ice-covered, and were now mis-firing seriously and overheating. To avoid serious damage, Alcock reduced the power from both the Rolls-Royce Eagles, and the aircraft glided back towards the Atlantic and, if Brown's navigation was correct, to the Irish coast.

Eventually they saw the ice start to slide from the airframe, rattling against the fuselage as it went. As the Vimy emerged into the clear air

Above: Air temperature decreases with height by 6½°C per km. Ice forms in clouds between 0°C and −40°C. A pilot can either descend into warm air or climb above the cloud.

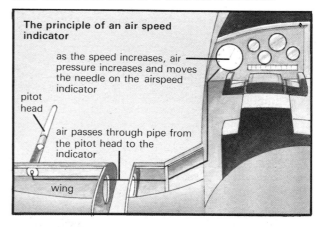

Above: Ice building up on the pitot head, causes the indicator to stick at the last reading before icing occurred. This can seriously mislead the pilot.

again, the engines responded and, his controls now back to normal, Alcock levelled the aircraft. The two men spotted the first dots of land – two islands off the coast of Ireland. A hurried check with the charts showed they were close to Galway Bay. They had crossed the Atlantic.

Their original plan was to fly on to Brooklands, close to London, but this was still several hundred kilometres away and the cloudbase was dangerously low. Both men were suffering from severe exhaustion after 16 hours in the air. They had had very little sleep before starting as they had been fully occupied preparing the Vimy in Newfoundland. In addition, having now conquered the Atlantic, they had no wish to crash on a Welsh mountain because of the cloudbase. Therefore when they crossed the coast at Clifden they decided to land in Ireland.

Above: The Vimy was finished too late for service in the First World War. The instrument panel was more complex than on earlier aircraft and had new blind-flying instruments.

Below: After its crash at Clifden, the Vimy was restored and is today displayed in the London Science Museum.

Alcock chose a long flat green field and came in for the landing. Despite his tiredness he put down the aircraft just where he wanted, but right at the last moment he realized he had made a mistake. The lush green grass was in fact a peat bog. The mainwheels of the Vimy dug in and the aircraft nosed over. As it shuddered to a halt Alcock and Brown scrambled triumphantly on to the wet earth. The Atlantic had been crossed non-stop.

The radio station at Clifden announced their success to the world and this remote corner of Ireland suffered an invasion of reporters and officials such as it had never seen before. Alcock and Brown were taken to London where they received their prize from Winston Churchill. Both were knighted, but sadly, Alcock had little time to enjoy his triumph. Six months later, in December 1919, he was killed in a flying accident over France while he was testing a new aeroplane.

31

Charles Lindbergh

The first solo flight across the Atlantic Ocean, 1927

Charles Augustus Lindbergh was born in 1902 in Detroit. His father's family were Swedish but they had changed their name from Mansson when they left Sweden for the 'New World' of the United States almost fifty years earlier.

Lindbergh's father was a lawyer and he had hoped that Charles would also take up law. Young Charles, later nicknamed 'Slim', was not a diligent student, however, and in 1922 he gave up college. He had already displayed a talent for engineering and in the 1920s the greatest challenge that posed was in the field of aviation. So Lindbergh invested most of his savings in a course of flying lessons.

He soon showed his talent as a pilot but no one would trust him with an aeroplane on the strength of a few flying lessons. So he did odd jobs around an airfield and worked as a stunt man, standing on the wing of aircraft flown at local air displays. He even did parachute jumps to raise money to buy his own aeroplane.

That ambition was achieved the following year when he took possession of a war-surplus trainer, a Curtiss JN-4, known as a 'Jenny', but that did not bring his dangerous stunts to an end. He earned a living 'barnstorming' (stunt flying) with the Jenny. The aeroplane was low-powered and not properly suited to aerobatics. Several times during the next year he crashed the plane, but each time he patched it up and was soon flying again. Then in 1924 he was selected by the US army as a flying cadet.

Confidence to tackle greater challenges

The army flying course was the first course in which Lindbergh ever did well in his studies. He graduated top of his class in the technical subjects, and in March 1925 he qualified as an army pilot. During his course he had made use of his parachuting experience by baling out of his aeroplane after a mid-air collision. He was the first pilot to parachute to safety after such an accident.

Left: 5,000 JN-4s were built by Curtiss in the US and most of America's airmen in the First World War learned to fly in them. They were not designed for aerobatics and Lindbergh's stunts in the Jenny could well have been disastrous.

When he could not get a job as a pilot, Lindbergh found even more dangerous employment as a stuntman with a flying circus.

Once qualified, Lindbergh joined the reserve of the air service in the rank of second lieutenant, and he returned to commercial flying. With the experience and the discipline gained from the army flying course, he obtained work more easily and he was involved in setting up the US airmail service. The long flights alone through the night, often in bad weather, gave him the confidence to tackle greater challenges. Twice after flying into fog when his fuel was running low, however, he was forced to abandon the aircraft by parachute.

In 1926 a New York hotel owner named Raymond Orteig renewed his offer of a prize of $25,000 to the first man to fly the Atlantic between New York and Paris. Though Lindbergh was only 25 years old he felt he could make the trip alone, provided he could get financial support and the right aeroplane. Finding the first of these was difficult; finding the second seemed impossible. Lindbergh was known as 'the flying fool' because of the many dangerous stunts he had performed, and his talk of a solo Atlantic crossing only reinforced his reputation. Lindbergh persevered, planning to fly St Louis–New York–Paris, and the businessmen of St Louis provided backing for the venture. His plane, which he called *Spirit of St Louis*, was specially built for him by Ryan Airlines Inc., a small manufacturer which was staking its future on the success of the project.

Careful preparations

The *Spirit of St Louis* was a high-winged monoplane powered by a Wright J-5 Whirlwind radial engine developing 220 horsepower. The aircraft was a refinement of the Ryan M-2, with extra fuel tanks and a wing span increased to 14 metres. Its range was 6,400 kilometres, and its most unusual feature was that the pilot had no forward view. The area in front of the cockpit was occupied by a fuel tank, and to see ahead for take-off and landing Lindbergh had to use a periscope.

After two months the aircraft was completed and Lindbergh began testing it immediately. Several other aviators were also aiming for the Orteig prize, and something of a race developed between people wanting to be the first to make the attempt.

In May 1927 Lindbergh set off from the Ryan factory in San Diego on the first leg of his journey across the Rocky Mountains to St Louis. En route he encountered similar engine icing problems to those which had bothered Alcock and Brown almost ten years earlier. He arrived at Roosevelt airfield, New York, on 12 May, having wasted little time in St Louis, and there he fitted an air intake heater to overcome the icing. But shortly after his arrival in New York the weather over the Atlantic deteriorated, ruling out any attempt to reach Paris. Lindbergh continued his careful preparations, as did his two rivals, Commander Byrd and his crew with the giant Fokker, and Levine and Chamberlin with a Bellanca. They were all made more cautious by the news that the Frenchmen Nungesser and Coli were missing while attempting to fly *from* Paris *to* New York – against the prevailing winds.

Above: Two weeks after Lindbergh's crossing, his rivals, Chamberlin and Levine, flew their Bellanca, *Miss Columbia*, from New York to Eisleben in Germany, and later continued to Croydon, England. Admiral Byrd and his crew later made the crossing, but none of these detracted from Lindbergh's achievement in crossing the Atlantic alone.

Radial engines, such as the Wasp, used the airflow over the cylinders to cool the engine, and did not require radiators and liquid cooling.

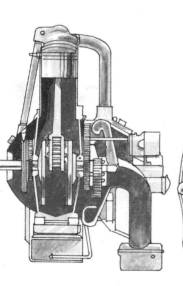

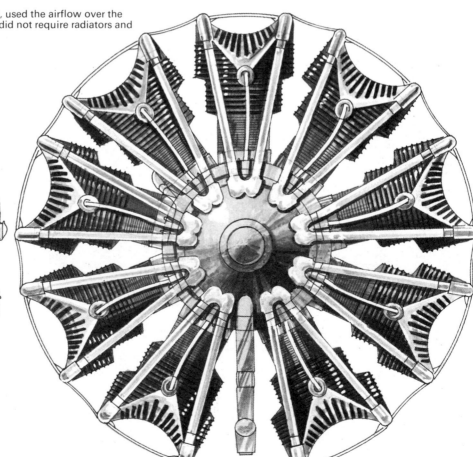

Left: Other pilots complained of the Ryan's heavy controls and complete lack of stability, but Lindbergh managed to fly it for $33\frac{1}{2}$ hours across the Atlantic.

The weather improves

On the evening of Thursday 19 May, Lindbergh and some friends had intended to go to the theatre as the weather was still poor. However, a routine telephone check with the weather office showed that the storm systems over the ocean were clearing rapidly and that the Atlantic weather should remain good for the next few days. At once the ground crew swung into action, checking and refuelling the aircraft. Lindbergh tried in vain to get some sleep. Early next morning he went out to the airfield where the *Spirit of St Louis* had been towed to the runway.

The grass was soft and wet after the continuous rain of the previous days. The aircraft was far heavier than ever before because of the large amount of fuel carried, so the take-off would be more difficult. At the end of the airstrip were telegraph wires 12 metres high and the take-off had to be carefully judged to clear them. To

The take-off was the most dangerous part of the flight.

assist him Lindbergh had placed a white flag at the side of the runway. If, when he reached the flag, he was not satisfied with his acceleration he would abandon the take-off, but after he had passed the marker he could not stop safely.

As the *Spirit of St Louis* began to roll, Lindbergh's friends at the airfield were very anxious,

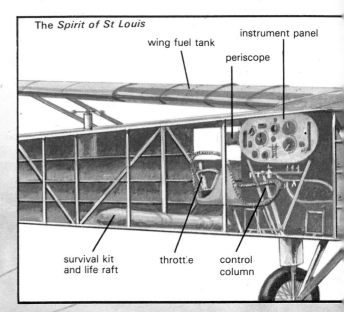

The *Spirit of St Louis*

wing fuel tank

instrument panel

periscope

survival kit and life raft

throttle

control column

and two of them took a fire extinguisher to the end of the runway in anticipation of a crash. But they need not have worried. The little monoplane, with its Wright Whirlwind engine developing its full 220 horsepower, lifted into the air after a very long run and cleared the telegraph wires by at least 10 metres.

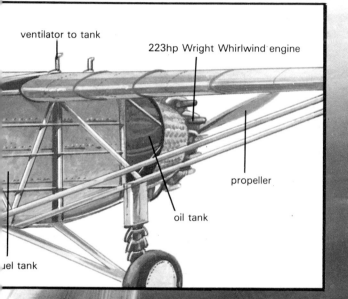

ventilator to tank

223hp Wright Whirlwind engine

propeller

oil tank

uel tank

Lindbergh flew low over the coast out to sea. His next navigation check would be hundreds of kilometres away over Nova Scotia because he did not carry a sextant to plot his position. When he reached Newfoundland he altered course to fly directly over the town of St John's so that he would have an exact position fix before setting course over the Atlantic.

He flew over banks of cloud which blocked the horizon ahead, and climbed over each layer until finally he could go no higher. He tightened his seat belt and flew on into the next darkened mass of cloud, soon feeling the aeroplane tossed about in the air currents. When he saw pellets of ice and hail streaming past the cabin windows he realized the danger of the aircraft icing up, and when he shone his torch on the wing his fears were confirmed. The spars of the wing and its leading edge were covered with a transparent coating of ice. This not only added weight to the already laden

Ice increased the drag and the weight of the aeroplane.

craft, but also reduced the lift generated by the wing. If this continued, the aircraft would soon be forced down towards the ocean, so Lindbergh reversed his course and flew back in search of the clear air he had left. He eventually burst out of the cloud, pointing back towards Newfoundland, and flew a slow turn to resume his track towards Paris. From then on he avoided the towering clouds and flew around them.

Exactly on course

As night fell, tiredness became his greatest enemy. Even flying with all the cabin windows open he was never far from sleep, but the night was short so far north, and flying towards the rising sun reduced the hours of darkness still further. When at last the sun broke through the early morning mist Lindbergh took the aircraft

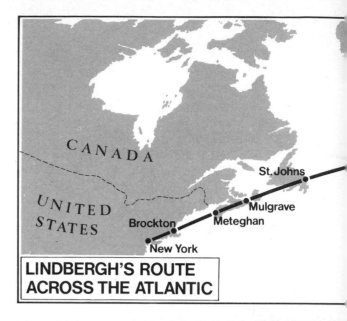

LINDBERGH'S ROUTE ACROSS THE ATLANTIC

The darkened runway in Paris was illuminated by the headlamps of cars. They had been driven from the city when the news spread that Lindbergh had been seen over England and was approaching his destination.

38

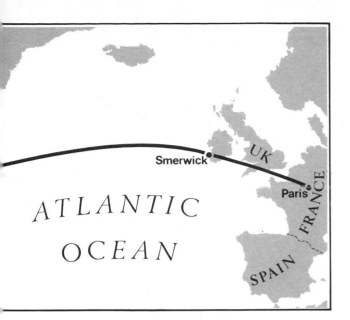

ATLANTIC OCEAN

Smerwick

Paris

UK

FRANCE

SPAIN

On his return to New York, Lindbergh was welcomed as a hero and was given the traditional 'ticker tape' reception.

down to just 3 metres above the waves in an effort to break the monotony.

He first realized that land must be near when he flew over some fishing boats. With the engine at low power he flew over the boats, only a few metres above them, and shouted, 'Which way to Ireland?' The fishermen didn't seem to understand and made no reply. However, after a few more kilometres the Irish coast could be seen on the horizon, and when he crossed it Lindbergh saw from his map that he was over Dingle Bay and exactly on course after nearly 30 hours of flight. When he had taken off he had not been sure if he would cross over Ireland at all as he might have been drawn as far off course as Norway or Portugal. He was therefore amazed and overjoyed to find himself within a few kilometres of the course charted in St Louis months before.

As he flew over Ireland and across the Irish Sea towards Cornwall in England, news of his progress reached France, and soon the roads towards Paris's airfield at Le Bourget were jammed by people who wanted to see Lindbergh's arrival. Shortly after the *Spirit of St Louis* crossed the French coast, darkness fell, but guided by the lights of Paris and the beacons that were lit to show pilots the way, Lindbergh flew on to the airfield. As he passed over the darkened countryside he saw a pool of light illuminating the touchdown zone of the runway, but beyond that was darkness. Any misjudgement during the landing would take the aircraft into that black area beyond the lights, which he could see were the headlamps of cars parked along the runway.

Because of the many hours of sleeplessness, and the tedium of droning alone across the Atlantic, Lindbergh found his senses numbed. He 'floated' just above the runway for a long way and the aircraft touched down just before the end of the lights. When he had slowed the aircraft sufficiently to turn back towards the hangars, Lindbergh was amazed to see a great crowd of people rushing forward to greet him. To avoid injuring anyone he cut the engine, but as the propeller stopped, the roar of the motor was replaced by that of the crowd chanting his name.

Overnight, Lindbergh had changed from an unknown airmail pilot into a world-famous celebrity. He was received in triumph by the kings and queens of Europe and given a hero's welcome on his return to the USA. Later in life he became a much-respected adviser on aviation matters, but he never again knew such adulation as he received at Le Bourget from the ordinary people of France.

Charles Kingsford Smith

*The first flight across
the Pacific Ocean, 1928*

When the First World War ended, an Australian by the name of Charles Kingsford Smith became, like many of his wartime colleagues, an unemployed pilot. During the war he had been promoted from a motorcycle despatch rider, eventually becoming an officer and a pilot who was respected for his flying ability. For his bravery he had been awarded the Military Cross, but he was only one of many men who had the award and so it did not help him to find work.

During 1919, Alcock and Brown crossed the Atlantic and inspired many airmen, including Kingsford Smith, to make further pioneering flights. The Australian government offered a £10,000 prize for the first flight between Britain and Australia, but to his disappointment Kingsford Smith was judged too inexperienced to take part. By the time the prize had been won by another two Australians, Ross and Keith Smith, Charles Kingsford Smith had a dangerous job in Hollywood, USA, stunt flying for films.

When he returned to Australia in 1921 he worked for several of the small airlines which were just starting up. His ambition to pioneer new air routes was not dead, and he met up with another Australian wartime pilot, Charles Ulm. Ulm had similar ideas, so together they started to plan ways of raising interest in a venture they had both been considering for some time – the crossing of the Pacific.

Plans are made

In 1927 they made a record-breaking flight round Australia, completing the 12,000 kilometres in just over ten days. During the resulting publicity they announced their plans for the Pacific crossing. Several people, and the Australian government, came forward with offers of financial help so Kingsford Smith and Ulm sailed for San Francisco, USA, the starting point for their journey.

They had not yet found the right aircraft for such a hazardous trip. The original idea was to use a Ryan monoplane, similar to that used by Lindbergh for the Atlantic crossing. This aircraft was eventually rejected on safety grounds because it only had a single engine, and because it was unsuitable for carrying the new navigational equipment.

After examining the other aircraft available, Kingsford Smith and Ulm decided on the Fokker F.VIIb trimotor, a type already proved on such trips as Admiral Byrd's flight over the North Pole in 1926. They were offered a Fokker, without engines, by the Australian polar explorer, Sir Hubert Wilkins, and arranged for three Wright Whirlwind engines to be fitted. These engines were in very short supply but Kingsford Smith was a resourceful man and managed to obtain three which were originally intended for the US navy. They were the same type of engine as Lindbergh had used in the *Spirit of St Louis,* and the combination of the Whirlwinds and the Fokker airframe produced one of the most reliable aircraft available.

The Australians still did not have enough money to finance the trip, and in order to gain the necessary support for it, they tried to break the world endurance record for flying. They made five attempts in all from a military airfield outside San Francisco, and on the last one were forced to give up after 50 hours in the air – less than 3 hours short of the record.

Start of the flight

They were broke and on the point of selling the aircraft when a rich Californian stepped in, offering to buy the machine and to finance their flight. Preparations for the journey were completed quickly. The structure of the aircraft was strengthened, and extra fuel tanks added; powerful radios were fitted and the aircraft and engines were given a thorough overhaul. Kingsford Smith arranged for hacksaws to be carried so that if they were forced to land on the sea the engines and fuselage could be cut away from the wooden wing, which could then be used as a life raft. Waterproof emergency supplies were installed in the wing, which was typical of Kingsford Smith's foresight and attention to detail.

The Fokker, now named *Southern Cross,* took off from Oakland airfield, San Francisco, on 31 May 1928. Kingsford Smith and Ulm were pilot and co-pilot, and two Americans, Harry Lyon and James Warner, were navigator and radio man. The first leg over the 4,000 kilometres of ocean to Wheeler Field, Honolulu, was trouble-free and almost monotonous. The weather was perfect throughout the 27-hour trip, but the crew knew it would be unlikely to remain so for the rest of the flight.

The next leg was the longest, and possibly the most difficult part of the journey. The conditions over the West Pacific were unpredictable, and the destination was Suva, an island of the Fiji islands, 5,000 kilometres away. Kingsford Smith had made arrangements to land on the local sports ground as there was no airfield in the Fiji islands and no aircraft had ever landed there.

Kingsford Smith preferred to land the aircraft on prepared runways, as sand strips could conceal hazards such as half-buried stones, but once he had checked the ground himself, both at Honolulu and at Suva, he moved the *Southern Cross* to the longer natural beach runways for the heavily laden take-off.

Supplies of fuel, oil and spare parts for the *Southern Cross* had to be sent in advance by sea to the islands which were used as stepping stones on the flight to Australia.

THE RECORD BREAKING FLIGHT ROUND AUSTRALIA

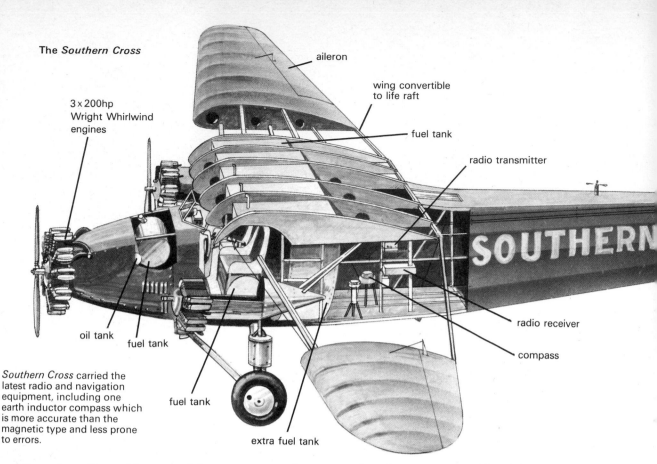

The *Southern Cross*

aileron

wing convertible
to life raft

fuel tank

radio transmitter

3 x 200hp
Wright Whirlwind
engines

SOUTHERN

oil tank

fuel tank

radio receiver

compass

Southern Cross carried the
latest radio and navigation
equipment, including one
earth inductor compass which
is more accurate than the
magnetic type and less prone
to errors.

fuel tank

extra fuel tank

The take-off on this second leg was at maximum weight, so, before filling up with fuel, the *Southern Cross* was flown across to another nearby island, Kanai, where a longer runway had been prepared at Barking Sands.

Problems in flight

No problems were encountered on this occasion, but while in flight the crew became worried by a troublesome engine and what they suspected was a fuel leak. To avoid several severe storms they had to alter course, and there were heavy rain squalls which soon had the crew and the aircraft soaked through. The radio also failed for a time, and Kingsford Smith and his navigator, Harry Lyon, were reduced to passing notes with compass directions and estimated times of arrival (ETAs) scribbled upon them. Their problems gradually disappeared as they flew closer to Suva. The fuel leak turned out to be condensation forming on the fuel lines, the engine cleared itself, and despite the course alterations Lyon's navigation brought them over Suva, where they made a safe landing on Albert Park Sports Ground. Rather to Kingsford Smith's surprise and relief, the ground had been cleared and prepared for their arrival just as he had requested.

Once again, after the crew had checked for hidden hazards, the *Southern Cross* was moved

to a beach runway at Naselai Beach. Captain Kingsford Smith's organizing talents were stretched to the full by the problems of transporting fuel to the beach. It was 30 kilometres from the main town, and take-off for the last leg to Brisbane was delayed until 8 June. This was the shortest stage, and the weather forecast was good when they took off. Just after darkness fell, however, they ran into a series of storms which almost forced the trimotor into the sea. At times the combined strength of Kingsford Smith and Ulm was needed to pull back the control column to prevent the *Southern Cross* from plunging to disaster.

Shortly after dawn the worst of the storm died away and, although the main compass had failed, Lyon felt sure they were not far off course. They crossed the Australian coast not far from Brisbane, where they landed to a hero's welcome on 9 June.

Kingsford Smith intended to pioneer air routes which would later be operated by scheduled airlines. Then in 1928, along with Ulm, he made the first air crossing of the Tasman Sea, between Australia and New Zealand. When he returned to Australia he started his own airline, called Australian National Airlines (ANA), which was equipped with versions of *Southern Cross* constructed by Avro in England. Kings-

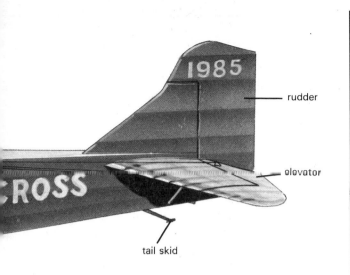

rudder

elevator

tail skid

Top right: Interior of *Southern Cross*. Centre right: Instrument panel. Bottom right: Chronometer and radio. The equipment carried aboard the *Southern Cross* may look primitive but in 1928 it was the best available. The instrument panel included a turn indicator and a large bowl compass but Kingsford Smith relied on his navigator, Harry Lyons, who had the new inductor compass, and on James Warner, the radio operator, who would obtain position reports when they were closer to land.

ford Smith flew *Southern Cross* to England to place the orders, then flew on across the Atlantic and eventually arrived back in San Francisco to complete the round-the-world trip.

About this time, ill-luck began to dog the Australian. He was still setting records, especially on the England–Australia routes, but one of ANA's aircraft was lost flying between Sydney and Melbourne. The contracts ANA hoped to get for carrying mail were won by another Australian airline, Queensland and Northern Territories Air Services (QANTAS). In 1931 ANA went bankrupt.

Sadly, Ulm died in 1934, flying from San Francisco to Honolulu, on a proving flight before setting up his own airline service.

By 1935 even Kingsford Smith's flying luck seemed to have deserted him. He was flying *Southern Cross* on its last trip from Australia to New Zealand, with Sir Gordon Taylor as co-pilot, when, several hundred kilometres out, flying in bad weather and at low level, the starboard engine failed. The *Southern Cross* could maintain height on the two remaining engines, but while the craft was still a long way from land, the port engine began to lose oil pressure and seemed certain to fail, which would send the aircraft into the sea. In the same way as Arthur Whitten Brown had done on the first Atlantic crossing,

Above: *Lady Southern Cross.* Kingsford-Smith entered this aircraft in the MacRobertson air race to Australia but was judged ineligible to compete.

VH-USB

VH

Honolulu

FIRST TRANS-PACIFIC FLIGHT

Suva

Brisbane

Sydney

Blenheim
Christchurch

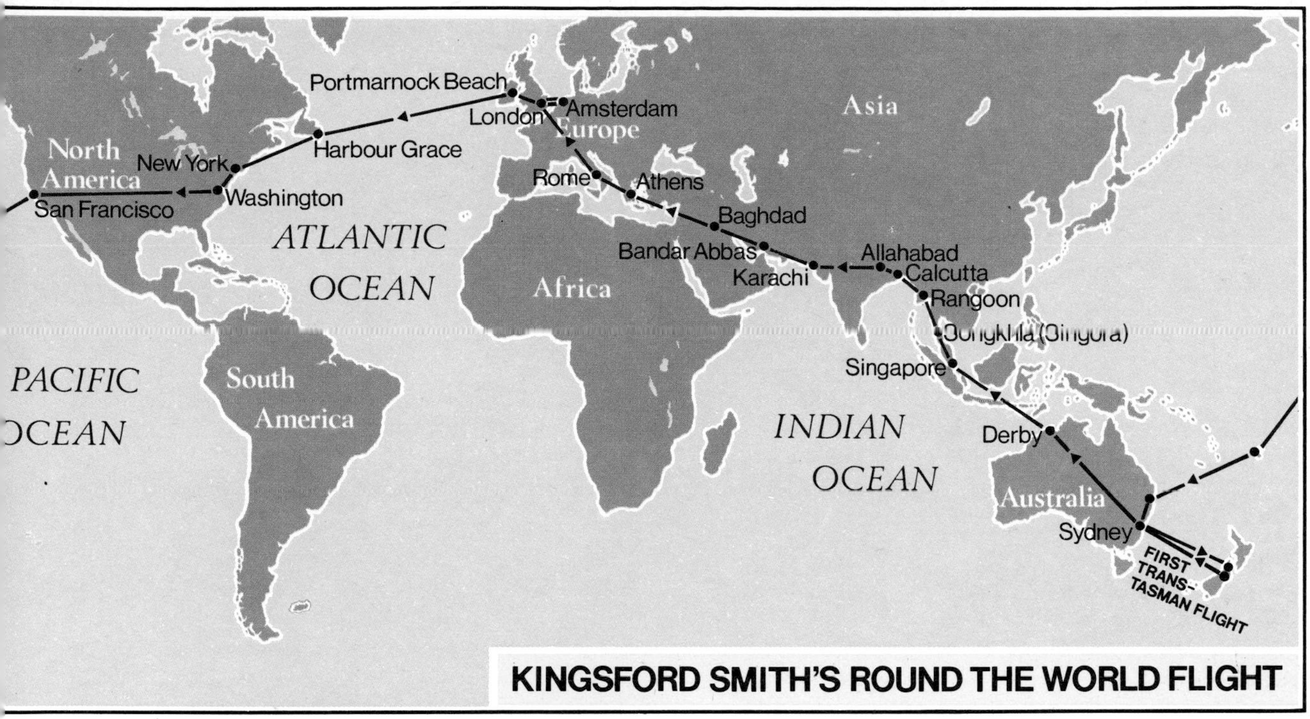
Portmarnock Beach
London
Amsterdam
Europe
Asia
North America
New York
Harbour Grace
Washington
San Francisco
Rome
Athens
Baghdad
ATLANTIC OCEAN
Bandar Abbas
Allahabad
Karachi
Calcutta
Africa
Rangoon
Singapore
PACIFIC OCEAN
South America
INDIAN OCEAN
Derby
Australia
Sydney
FIRST TRANS-TASMAN FLIGHT
KINGSFORD SMITH'S ROUND THE WORLD FLIGHT

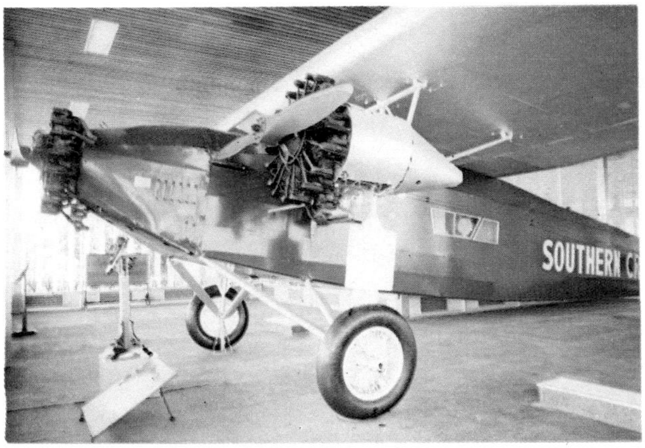
SOUTHERN C

Above: *Southern Cross* has been restored to its condition at the time of the Pacific flight and is displayed at Brisbane Airport, where Kingsford Smith and his crew landed.

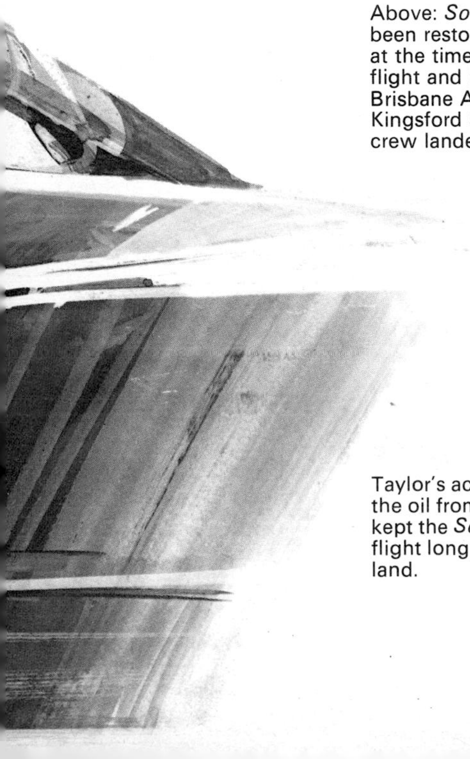

Taylor's action in transferring the oil from the failed engine, kept the *Southern Cross* in flight long enough to reach land.

Gordon Taylor climbed out on to the wing strut beside the failed starboard engine. He drained off some of its oil into a Thermos flask, and then poured it into an empty suitcase in the cockpit. When he had enough oil in the suitcase he climbed out and transferred the much-needed liquid to the faltering port engine. He made six such trips transferring the oil, before the *Southern Cross* reached safety.

What was left of Kingsford Smith's luck did not last much longer. In November 1935 he took off from Lympne in England intending to make a record-breaking flight to Australia. He was flying a Lockheed Altair named *Lady Southern Cross* which he had used for an Australia to USA crossing. This flight was a desperate move to regain the public's confidence in him, and it was not planned with the foresight Kingsford Smith had shown in the past. Between Rangoon and Singapore, *Lady Southern Cross* went missing. A thorough air–sea search was started immediately, but no trace was found until two years later when a wheel from the Lockheed was washed ashore.

ANA no longer exists, so the only memorial to Kingsford Smith is the *Southern Cross*. After being stored in a hangar for some years the Fokker was restored to its original condition and is now on show in a huge glass case at Eagle Farm Airport, Brisbane, where Kingsford Smith was given such a warm welcome after his flight across the Pacific.

Amy Johnson

A very determined lady, 1903–1941

Amy Johnson was rarely described as a good pilot. Her first flying instructor had a low opinion of her abilities, and her landings, though usually safe, were never of a consistently high standard. However, she was a very determined lady who made an impact as a pilot and engineer in the early thirties, at a time when few women managed to overcome the blatant bias against them in what was almost exclusively a male way of life.

Amy's schooldays in Hull were marked only by a certain tomboyishness, and a liking for vigorous sport. She had to have two false teeth when her front ones were knocked out by a cricket ball. She went on to take an Arts degree at Sheffield University and then to work as a typist in her home town.

The bright lights of London beckoned, but before she left Hull, Amy's first interest in aviation stirred when she and a friend paid five shillings (25p) each for a pleasure flight from an airfield near the town. Encouragement to leave for London came when a Swiss boyfriend took her to visit his parents in Switzerland. When she returned to Hull she found her birthplace too quiet and depressing. In 1927 she moved to London and took a job, first in a department store, then as a typist with a solicitor's firm. In 1928 her salary was £5 a week, so when she decided to learn to fly, the thirty shillings (£1.50) per hour charge for lessons must have been a severe drain on her resources.

Her first lessons at the London Aero Club were not a success. Because she was short of funds, and also because of the poor weather during the winter, there were long gaps between the lessons. It took more than 15 hours' flying before she was allowed to fly the Club's de Havilland Cirrus Moth, solo.

An interest in engineering

When she had flown solo, Amy developed her interest in engineering by making friends with the engineers who serviced the Club's aeroplanes. At the same time she continued with her flying and, in order to save money for lessons, she moved to cheap accommodation in Edgware,

close to the Stag Lane aerodrome, where she was learning. She soon gained her 'A' pilot's licence (like today's Private Pilot's licence) and while she worked towards her 'B' licence (the professional qualification), she spent her holiday working in the hangars in order to gain an engineer's licence.

There was considerable opposition from Club members to another member, especially a woman, working in the hangars. However, Amy had the support of the chief engineer, a man named Jack Humphreys, who became her guide and a strong support during the adventures she faced in the future. In 1928, a man named Bert Hinkler flew a light aircraft solo to Australia in less than 16 days, and Amy resolved that she would attempt to break that record. If she were successful she would help the cause of the British light aircraft industry, and greatly assist women pilots to be taken seriously by their male colleagues.

Amy had no money, no aeroplane and very little experience, but her determination made up for these. After approaching many important people with little success she was helped by Sir Sefton Brancker, the Director of Civil Aviation, to win the support of Lord Wakefield, the wealthy director of an oil company. Her father also lent her money to buy a de Havilland Gipsy Moth which she painted dark green, her lucky colour, and named *Jason*.

Jason had previously been used for long trips so was already fitted with extra fuel tanks to carry 360 litres of fuel – enough for 13 hours in the air. Amy carried spare parts, including a propeller, and emergency supplies in case she was forced to land in isolated areas. Thus equipped, the little biplane required a long runway to get airborne as it was heavy and was powered only by a 100-horsepower Gipsy engine. On her first attempt at a take-off on the trip to Australia, Amy decided the machine was not going to get into the air, and she managed to stop it before it hit the boundary fence. The next attempt was more successful, and at 7.45 am on 5 May 1930, the tiny de Havilland struggled into the air from Croydon airfield in Surrey. Amy's attempt to break Bert Hinkler's record had begun.

Above and right: Amy Johnson made her mark in two male-dominated professions, first as an engineer, then as a pilot.

Left: Besides the spare parts for *Jason*, Amy's emergency kit included food and drink, and a revolver with which to protect herself.

An eventful journey

The first flight was to Vienna, and apart from a petrol leak which made Amy feel ill from the fumes, it was without serious incident. However, when she got to Constantinople (Istanbul) the next day, Turkish customs officials impounded both Amy and *Jason* until some desperate telephone calls produced the documents for their release. During the next days, Amy came very close to some Turkish mountains while trying to fly below storm clouds. She then had to make a forced landing in the middle of a desert in the Middle East after flying into a dust storm.

When Amy arrived in Baghdad, the undercarriage of her aircraft collapsed because the desert landing had strained it badly, and a spar sheared on landing. A new spar was soon produced, and repairs made, but this was only the first damage *Jason* suffered during the trip. At Bandar Abbas the undercarriage again collapsed; when Amy landed on a parade ground in India, the Moth came to rest jammed between two buildings, with a damaged wing. At Rangoon, she again missed the airfield and landed on a sports field where *Jason* suffered a broken undercarriage and propeller, and damaged wing.

With the help of the staff and pupils from the local technical college Amy patched up her aircraft. At first it had seemed impossible to find canvas for the repairs, until one of the team produced a pile of canvas shirts – actually made from aeroplane fabric left over from the First World War. The shirts were re-cycled and Amy set off again. At Singapore a new wing was fitted, then on the landing at Java, again some distance from the airfield, the canvas on the wing was torn by bamboo stakes marking a building site where Amy had landed. *Jason* was taken to Sourabaya where the propeller was again replaced, as it had been damaged by the monsoon rains.

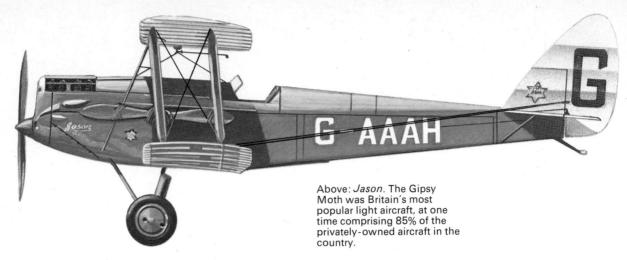

Above: *Jason*. The Gipsy Moth was Britain's most popular light aircraft, at one time comprising 85% of the privately-owned aircraft in the country.

Despite all these troubles, Amy landed safely at Darwin, Australia, on 24 May, 20 days after leaving Croydon. A few days later she crashed on landing at Brisbane. *Jason* was taken back to England by sea for repairs, but Amy was unhurt and continued with a triumphant tour of Australia. Because of the delays caused by the damage to the aircraft (since leaving Croydon two propellers, three undercarriages and a wing had been replaced), Amy did not beat the record for the journey. However, her efforts to overcome the problems she faced had attracted the attention of newspapers all over the world. When she returned to England she had become a major celebrity, welcomed by large crowds wherever she went. She also made a large sum of money and was given two aeroplanes.

The strain of being in the public eye

Stardom did not appeal to Amy. She cancelled the British tour a newspaper had arranged for her, but her health deteriorated because of the strain of being constantly in the public eye. She entered a nursing home for a while, and then had a period of complete rest. When she was fit again she embarked on another solo flight, this time to China.

She left London in January, but several times became completely lost. Eventually she crashed in Poland, once again escaping unhurt. Amy's sheer determination to succeed eventually triumphed. That summer she and her old friend and mechanic, Jack Humphreys, flew her de Havilland Puss Moth across Europe and Asia to Tokyo. By this time, however, the newspapers were full of other epic flights and little attention was paid to her trip. Amy resolved to make her next flight a more dramatic effort so she decided to make an attempt on the round-the-world record.

In Rangoon, *Jason* was repaired with shirts, which had themselves been made from aircraft fabric.

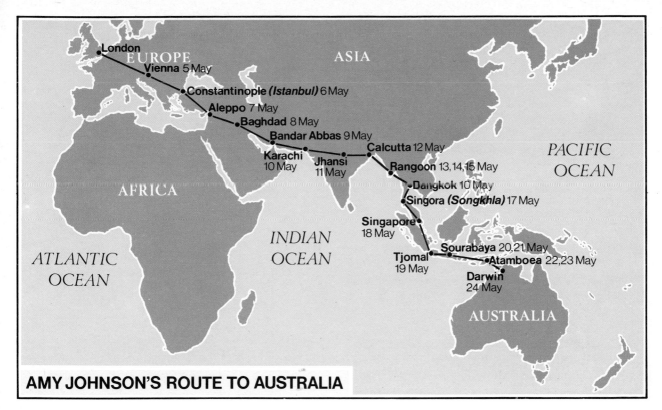

AMY JOHNSON'S ROUTE TO AUSTRALIA

Map labels:
- London
- Vienna 5 May
- Constantinople (*Istanbul*) 6 May
- Aleppo 7 May
- Baghdad 8 May
- Bandar Abbas 9 May
- Karachi 10 May
- Jhansi 11 May
- Calcutta 12 May
- Rangoon 13, 14, 15 May
- Bangkok 10 May
- Singora (*Songkhla*) 17 May
- Singapore 18 May
- Tjomal 19 May
- Sourabaya 20, 21 May
- Atamboea 22, 23 May
- Darwin 24 May

EUROPE · ASIA · PACIFIC OCEAN · AFRICA · INDIAN OCEAN · ATLANTIC OCEAN · AUSTRALIA

Before this flight could take place, Amy again fell ill. To recuperate she took a sea cruise to South Africa, where she met Jim Mollison. Mollison was also a pioneering airman with some notable flights to his credit. He and Amy had met briefly in Australia, but when they returned from South Africa they saw each other frequently and they were married in July 1932. The marriage of two well-known aviators excited public attention, and Amy's name was once again in the headlines, especially when she and Jim attempted to break the world's long-distance record by flying from New York to Baghdad. They had a new twin-engined aeroplane built by de Havilland, but even before they reached New York they were in trouble, when the undercarriage collapsed as they were taking off from Croydon.

Jim blamed the rough ground for the accident and decided to make the next attempt from the flat sands of Pendine Beach in Wales. To relieve the strain on the undercarriage the fuel load for the flight to New York was kept to a minimum, but after crossing the Atlantic safely they found the petrol was running low. Jim was a stubborn man, and although he could have landed safely at several airfields he pressed on towards New York. Darkness was falling and when they were 80 kilometres from their destination the fuel ran out. The biplane crashed into a marsh and they had to give up the record-breaking attempt.

Amazing determination

The following year they flew one of the new de Havilland Comets in the MacRobertson race from England to Australia. Three Comets were entered and they were the only British hopes of beating the American aircraft that were present.

The Mollisons' aircraft was painted black and named *Black Magic* as black was Jim's favourite colour, but it brought them little luck. Although they were in the lead at Karachi, they first lost their way, then refuelled the aircraft with ordinary motor car petrol by mistake. Finally an engine failed, and they were forced to withdraw from the race, which was won by Charles Scott and Tom Campbell Black in another Comet.

After this fiasco, Amy and Jim's marriage broke up. Amy hoped to make a living as an agent for the American Beechcraft aeroplane company. She ordered one of their touring aeroplanes, but it was damaged in another landing crash after she failed to wind down properly the retractable undercarriage. She then attempted to regain the record for the London–Cape Town flight which she first held soon after her Australia trip. She borrowed another Beechcraft but soon removed the wheels from that one on landing. A British manufacturer named Percival lent her a Percival Gull for the next attempt. She reached North Africa without incident but on the next take-off the machine swung round on the stony runway and the undercarriage collapsed.

Once again Amy displayed her amazing courage and determination. She flew back to England by scheduled airline and then returned, flying another aircraft carrying spare parts and a mechanic. Within a month of her first attempt she returned to England with the Gull and took off to try again. This time she not only set a record for the London–Cape Town flight, but also set one for the return trip.

Difficulties in finding a job

Amy was welcomed in Europe as a heroine, but she was living well beyond her means and her money problems meant she had to sell her aeroplane and many personal possessions. She tried to get a job as a professional pilot but again came up against the heavy discrimination against women which existed in flying. She had more than 2,000 hours' flying experience but nobody would give her a job. She made some money from writing books and newspaper articles about her experiences and then, with war looming, she was offered a flying job with a small aviation company on the south coast of England. After flying for

Above: There were no facilities for aircraft at Pendine Sands and all the fuel was loaded by hand from barrels.
Below: The de Havilland Comet was produced specially for the MacRobertson race to Australia. One of the three entered won the race, flown by Scott and Campbell Black.

50

Top: After the undercarriage collapsed at Croydon, Amy and Jim made their next attempt to fly *Seafarer* to America from Pendine Sands in Wales. They hoped that the smooth beach would be less of a strain on the undercarriage than was Croydon's grass runway.

Above: The Airspeed Oxford was a military development of the civil Airspeed Envoy. During the war more than 8,000 Oxfords were built as advance trainers for the RAF and normally, a crew of three was carried. Amy was flying an Oxford when she crashed into the Thames.

twelve years she was at last earning her living as a commercial pilot. A few months later, however, the outbreak of war brought an end to her new job, and Amy volunteered to join a new organization called Air Transport Auxiliary (ATA). They were responsible for ferrying military aircraft to the Royal Air Force (RAF) stations.

This was a responsible task which was undertaken by pilots who were ineligible for the RAF, and there were several women members. Amy enjoyed the work and was very popular when she arrived at the RAF aerodromes. She was frequently surrounded by crowds of airmen asking for her autograph. Although the ATA pilots were not involved in combat, they flew military aircraft without radio and were often pounced upon by enemy fighters. They flew in poor weather, without navigators, and several brave pilots died.

In January 1941 Amy took off from Squires Gate airfield near Blackpool on ATA work. She was flying an Airspeed Oxford twin-engined training aircraft to Kidlington airfield. She had spent the previous night at her sister's house in Blackpool after bad weather had forced her to break her journey from Prestwick. The weather was still poor when she took off from Blackpool, and the south of England was under a cover of cloud. That afternoon the aircraft fell into the Thames estuary. Amy was seen falling from it but her body was never recovered.

Irene Jevans

A journey with Imperial Airways, 1934

In the spring of 1934 Irene Jevans found herself in a position which, in those years of the depression, was all too common. After twenty years as governess to a well-to-do family in London, she was out of work. Her employer's children were now quite grown up, and he had agreed to recommend her to any of his friends who might require her services.

Shortly before Easter, Irene received a letter postmarked Khartoum, Africa. The writer, Major G. J. Sands, identified himself as a former colleague of her previous employer and went on to ask if she would be available for a period of three years to attend to the education of his two children. He had instructed Thomas Cook and Son to make any necessary travel arrangements, and if she accepted the post he would be delighted to see her in Khartoum as soon as possible. Irene had never been out of England but she was interested to see more of the Empire. She sat down at once and wrote a letter of acceptance.

Two weeks later, Miss Jevans was dropped by taxi at the Victoria terminal of Imperial Airways. She carried only a small case with clothes for the journey, as her trunks had been sent on in advance by sea. At the checking-in area the bags and passengers were weighed. The baggage allowance was 15 kilograms and any excess baggage, or even overweight passengers could affect the aeroplane's performance.

Once the formalities were completed, the passengers were led to an Imperial Airways' limousine for the drive to London's Croydon Airport in Surrey. On the journey, the five passengers spoke little but Irene discovered that only one man among them, a reserved civil servant, was completing the journey to Cape Town. The others were leaving at either Paris or Alexandria. At about 11.30 am, the limousine drew up outside the impressive new terminal at Croydon where the passengers were shown into a comfortable waiting room.

Until the Second World War, Croydon was Britain's major international airport, and among the biggest in the world.

THE ROUTE FROM LONDON TO CAPE TOWN

London
Paris
Brindisi
Athens
Mirabella
Alexandria
Cairo
Wadi Halfa
Khartoum
Kisumu
Salisbury
Johannesburg
Cape Town

The stewards of Imperial Airways were experienced in dealing with nervous travellers, as air travel was still a novelty in the 1930s.

The finest air service in the world

Horatius, registered G-AAXD, was one of Imperial Airways' fleet of four Handley Page HP.42 biplanes used on European services. They could seat 39 passengers, though Irene's flight had only 5 booked. Each aircraft cost £42,000 when bought in 1931 and they were among the safest airliners in the world. They were also among the slowest, but Imperial Airways compensated for that by providing the finest airborne service in the world. When Irene and her fellow travellers were led out to the aeroplane, it was surrounded by airline staff loading food and drink for the journey. Despite the imminent departure, no haste was shown. In fact, a directive from Imperial Airways instructed its staff never to hurry in the presence of passengers, as undue haste might panic a nervous passenger. By 12.30 pm, the scheduled departure time, all was ready. Each of the four Jupiter engines roared into life and the pilot taxied across Croydon's rough grass to the take-off point. The controller gave take-off clearance by flashing a green light from the control tower on top of the terminal building, and *Horatius* lumbered down the runway and into the air.

Soon after take-off, a white-coated steward served drinks and presented the passengers with a comprehensive luncheon menu. He explained which route they were taking and named the towns they were passing over. Irene did not want to go too close to the window because of the great height at which they were flying (about 500 metres), so she stayed close to the aisle and sipped a glass of wine.

By the time they crossed the English coast near Lympne, Miss Jevans had relaxed a little and was enjoying a chicken salad. However, when the steward tried to point out Brighton pier as they passed near it she still felt nervous when looking down. After a while though, she started to enjoy the scenery rolling past – the great white cliffs, and the boats tossed about by the waves in the Channel. The airline provided a map of the route and by following it, Irene could pick out the town of Abbeville on the French coast.

With so few passengers on board, the steward had time to talk about his early experiences with Imperial Airways and their predecessor, Handley Page Transport. He frightened Miss Jevans by telling her that on one London to Paris flight the aircraft was forced to land seventeen times and the journey took two days. In the mid-1920s some of the passengers sat in an open cabin and were issued with goggles and flying coats before take-off. Often the aeroplane was too heavy so the baggage was left behind to follow later. The pilot carried £10 'forced landing money', in case of a landing away from base, and also a list of relevant train timings to get the passengers to their destination. By the time *Horatius* landed at le Bourget Airport, Paris, Irene felt quite grateful for the solid comfort and safety of the HP.42 compared with earlier airliners.

From Le Bourget the passengers were transferred to a southbound express train which took them through France and Switzerland to Italy. This surface journey was necessary as the various governments involved could not come to agreement on a direct air service.

After two nights and a day the train reached the Italian port of Brindisi at about 4 am. In the grey light of dawn the passengers could distinguish the silver shape of *Sylvanus*, a Short Kent flying boat, moored alongside the boarding jetty. The bleary-eyed travellers were led into a small terminal building where they were served breakfast before boarding the aeroplane. The Kents had recently replaced the Calcutta flying boats on the Brindisi–Alexandria flight and were considered quite comfortable aeroplanes. They were slightly larger than the HP.42 in which Miss Jevans had flown to Paris and they were a little faster, with a maximum speed of 200 kph. They carried 16 passengers and a crew of 4.

On to Alexandria

At about 7 am the engines were run up to full power and in a great flurry of spray *Sylvanus* roared across the bay and into the air. Irene had chosen a window seat as she now had no fears about looking down, but she was quite alarmed during the take-off run when a great wall of sea water obscured the view. Once in the air, however, with the beautiful Adriatic Sea spreading towards the horizon, she began to enjoy the journey. The catering was not to the same standard as on *Horatius*, but the sandwiches and coffee served by the steward sufficed until Athens came into view. Before they landed, one of the crew told her an interesting story. Gold was often carried in the cabins of the flying boats in earlier years. This cargo survived various forced landings and other adventures until an ingot went missing on a flight from Alexandria to Athens. After a thorough investigation, the police found that just before landing at Athens the steward had tied the gold to a float and tossed it overboard to be recovered by an accomplice in a small boat.

Short Kent flying boat

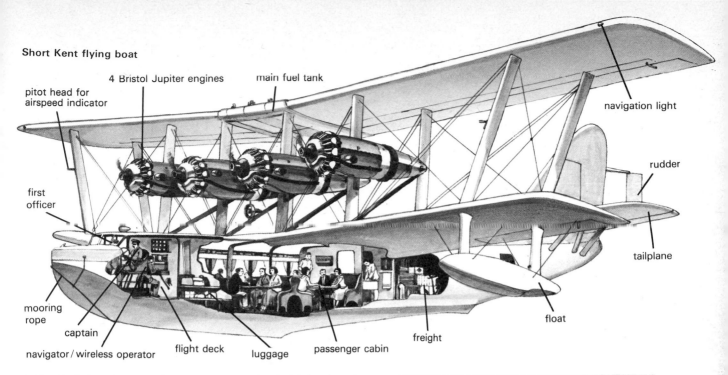

pitot head for airspeed indicator

4 Bristol Jupiter engines

main fuel tank

navigation light

rudder

tailplane

first officer

mooring rope

captain

navigator / wireless operator

flight deck

luggage

passenger cabin

freight

float

Specially designed wheels, called beaching gear, were attached to the flying-boats to bring them ashore for maintenance.

When the aircraft was in the water and afloat, the beaching gear was removed.

Imperial Airways offered a very high standard of catering, and their galleys were always well stocked.

In the featureless desert areas south of Cairo, the River Nile was the only landmark available and greatly assisted navigation on the route to Khartoum. Imperial Airways established several airfields along the river for use in an emergency. Most forced landings were caused by dust storms and freak weather conditions.

Irene spent a pleasant night in Athens, though she felt too tired for any sightseeing. In summer, when daylight lasted longer, the flying boat continued to Alexandria in one day, but on this occasion the passengers were quite happy to break the journey and escape from the non-stop roar of the motors for a few hours. The next morning they re-embarked and flew on to Alexandria with a re-fuelling stop at Mirabella in Crete. The great wave of spray which covered the windows on take-off and landing was still quite alarming, but otherwise Irene was enjoying the flying and considered herself quite an experienced air traveller.

On arrival at Alexandria, there was a little trouble with an Egyptian official over the baggage. One of the local Imperial Airways' staff went to find the pilot as he was responsible for his passengers and their baggage until they had cleared customs. He soon sorted out the problem and Irene joined the handful of passengers boarding the southbound aircraft, another HP.42. Imperial Airways used four HP.42s on African and Middle East routes. They differed from the European version in seating only 18 passengers, and they had an increased fuel capacity. Once again there were few passengers for the service, but Imperial Airways made their profit from the subsidy they received for carrying the mail. No subsidy was received, however, if the mail was more than 48 hours late.

The last stages

Horsa, as this latest aircraft was called, made only a short hop to Cairo where the passengers spent the night, before making an early take-off next morning. At Cairo the passengers were issued with Imperial Airways currency coupons. These came in five shillings (25p) and two shillings and sixpence (12½p) and were meant to avoid the continual changing of currencies. Originally they were exchanged for local currency, but soon most people in Egypt happily accepted them as cash.

The early morning was the best time for flying as the air was still cool, and not as bumpy as it became later in the day when the heat built up. After take-off the pilot flew low to give a good view of the pyramids before setting course for Khartoum. Irene was curious to know how the pilot would find his way, and the steward pointed out that he simply followed the River Nile all the

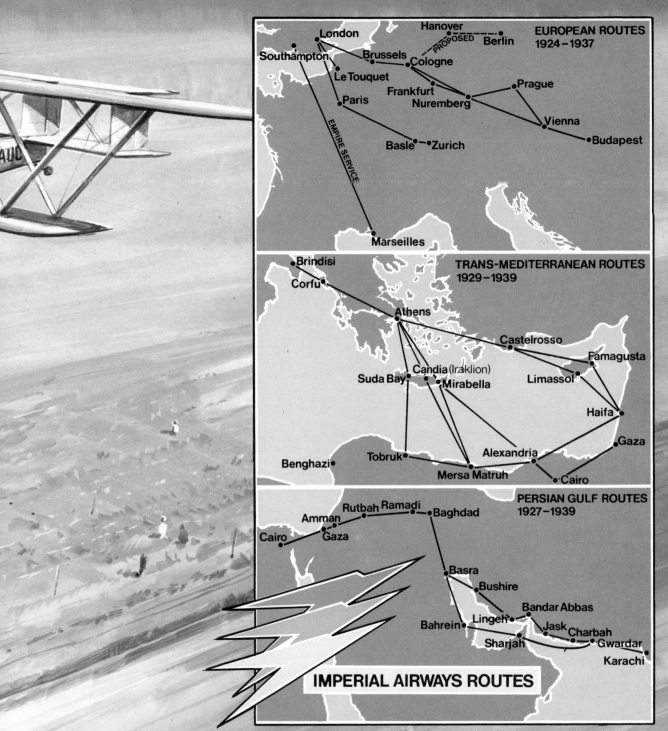

IMPERIAL AIRWAYS ROUTES

EUROPEAN ROUTES 1924–1937

London
Hanover
PROPOSED
Berlin
Southampton
Brussels
Cologne
Le Touquet
Frankfurt
Prague
Paris
Nuremberg
EMPIRE SERVICE
Vienna
Basle
Zurich
Budapest
Marseilles

TRANS-MEDITERRANEAN ROUTES 1929–1939

Brindisi
Corfu
Athens
Castelrosso
Famagusta
Candia (Iraklion)
Suda Bay
Mirabella
Limassol
Haifa
Gaza
Benghazi
Tobruk
Alexandria
Mersa Matruh
Cairo

PERSIAN GULF ROUTES 1927–1939

Amman
Rutbah
Ramadi
Baghdad
Cairo
Gaza
Basra
Bushire
Bandar Abbas
Bahrein
Lingeh
Jask
Charbah
Sharjah
Gwardar
Karachi

way. He explained that over the featureless desert between Cairo and Baghdad the RAF had ploughed a trench which the pilots could follow. Pilots always flew to the right of any lines they followed, such as the desert trench, railway lines or canals. They had done this ever since the first mid-air collision, between two aircraft in France which were flying in opposite directions on the same side of the Abbeville–Beauvais road.

With the advent of radio, which all Imperial

Airways' aeroplanes carried, it was more difficult to get lost, but Irene noticed that, just as the steward had told her earlier, the pilot usually kept the aeroplane within sight of the waters of the Nile.

After about five hours, they landed at Wadi Halfa to refuel. This was a desert airstrip where the passengers used to stop for the night until the introduction of the HP.42. These latest aircraft could fly from Cairo to Khartoum in one day, but

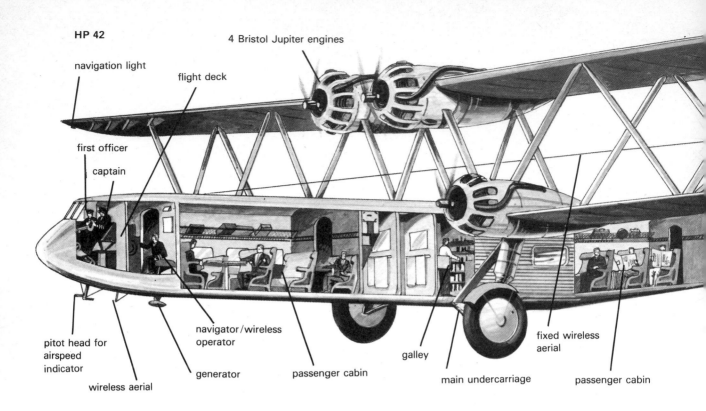

HP 42

navigation light

flight deck

4 Bristol Jupiter engines

first officer

captain

pitot head for airspeed indicator

wireless aerial

navigator/wireless operator

generator

passenger cabin

galley

main undercarriage

fixed wireless aerial

passenger cabin

the rest-house at Wadi Halfa was kept in case of an unscheduled stop. The airlines had to build rest-houses all over Africa, and in many of the less civilized areas they also built stockades to protect the aircraft and passengers from marauding tribesmen.

The passengers were given a light meal, while the pilot and his mechanic replenished the fuel and checked the oil and water. Within two hours they were in the air again, on the final leg of the journey to Khartoum. Two hours before they were due to land, a great dust storm rose up and the pilot, who could see only a short distance ahead, was forced to land on one of the many emergency landing grounds along the route. One group of travellers who had been stranded there for two days, laid out a golf course and organized a championship while they were waiting for help. *Horsa*, however, was able to take off after only an hour as the storm did not take long to clear, and she reached Khartoum just after nightfall. The pilot flew low over the airfield to alert the staff to light the flarepath which marked the runway. Then he made a good approach and landed.

Horsa continued to Cape Town the next morning, but Miss Jevans's adventure was over For the time being. She returned to her quiet life as a governess, though she often entertained her new charges with stories of her trip from London.

Below: The flight deck of the HP.42 was similar to present airliners, with two pilots side-by-side and the engine controls between them.

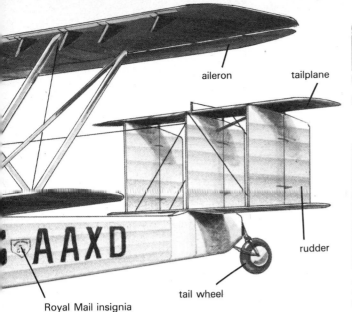

aileron

tailplane

E-AAXD

rudder

tail wheel

Royal Mail insignia

Above: Although voice radio communication was being developed, morse code was still in use, and the HP.42 carried a specialized radio operator.

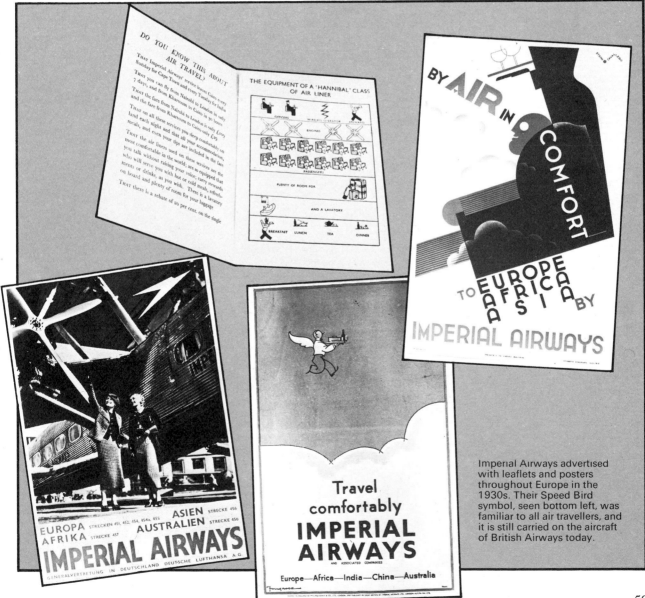

Imperial Airways advertised with leaflets and posters throughout Europe in the 1930s. Their Speed Bird symbol, seen bottom left, was familiar to all air travellers, and it is still carried on the aircraft of British Airways today.

Hugo Eckener

The pioneer of airship services,
1909–1937

Hugo Eckener was one of a small band of journalists and spectators gathered at Friedrichshafen on the shores of Lake Constance in southern Germany. It was 2 July 1900, and he had been commissioned by the *Frankfurter Zeitung*, a large German newspaper, to cover the demonstration by Count Ferdinand von Zeppelin of his rigid airship, called the LZ1.

The LZ1 was not a success and Eckener wrote an unenthusiastic piece for the newspaper, offering several criticisms. The most important criticism was that the airship's speed of 25 kph was not enough when the wind against which it was flying might easily be 40 kph or more. But Eckener, realizing the potential of the design, gave his support to the Count and eventually became the Zeppelin Company's publicity officer.

When LZ4, an airship ordered by the German army, was totally wrecked on landing, Eckener launched a public appeal for money to build a new airship, as the Count was almost bankrupt. The response was such, that within months the Count had set up a new company with sufficient funds to develop and build the most advanced airships in the world.

In 1909 another company, Deutsche Luftschiffahrts AG (DELAG), was founded to run commercial airship services and Hugo Eckener became Director of Flight Operations. In 1911 he received his airship captain's licence and immediately took command of LZ8, named *Deutschland II*. During the next few years Eckener pioneered airship services among all the major towns in Germany, and when war broke out in 1914, DELAG had carried 10,000 passengers on 1,500 flights and had never had an accident.

The German army and navy both valued the airship for military work and many zeppelins were built for reconnaissance and bombing missions. Eckener's role was that of test pilot and adviser, and he gained a fine reputation for his ability to train crews in handling the airships.

A zeppelin for America

When the war ended, Eckener took control of the Zeppelin Company as the Count had died in 1917. Once again the company was in a poor financial state but help came from an unusual direction. The Americans agreed to Eckener building a zeppelin for them instead of the company paying the monetary compensation it owed for several airships the crews had wrecked rather than hand them over to the allies.

The new airship, LZ126, was the biggest in the world at almost 200 metres long. In October 1924 she was ready for delivery to the United

The airship brought a luxury to air travel with which airliners could not compete, and the Graf Zeppelin was bigger than most of the ocean liners of its time.

States and on 13 October, with Hugo Eckener in command, the new airship lifted off from Friedrichshafen in perfect weather. Eighty hours later, after a completely trouble-free flight, Eckener brought her down to a safe landing at Lakehurst, New Jersey.

Back in Germany no funds could be raised in official quarters for another airship, so Eckener again turned to the German people. The appeal raised half a million pounds and the government eventually contributed the rest.

The *Graf Zeppelin* was 30 metres longer than the LZ126 and was powered by five 530-horsepower Maybach engines. Her top speed was 120 kph and she could carry 20 passengers. In October 1928 Eckener was ready to operate passenger flights across the Atlantic, but bad weather prevailed along the route. After a day's delay Eckener decided to set off using a southerly route to avoid the worst of the weather. Two days out, in the middle of the Atlantic and with no

After crossing Russia, the *Graf Zeppelin* arrived over Tokyo on its world tour.

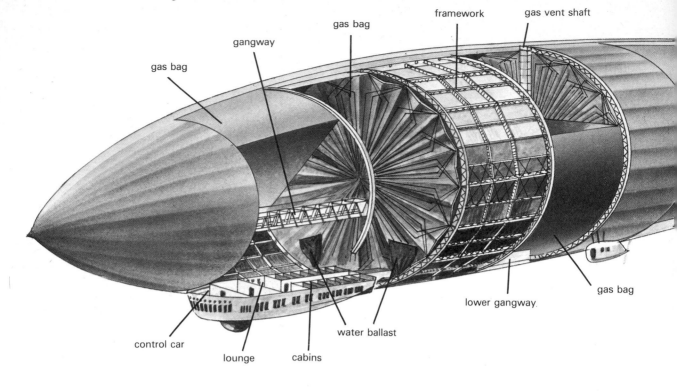

gas bag

gangway

gas bag

framework

gas vent shaft

control car

lounge

cabins

water ballast

lower gangway

gas bag

Below: All airships were susceptible to winds. Earlier airships had a maximum speed through the air of 35 kph. If they flew against a head wind of 40 kph they went backwards at 5 kph.

Below: Airships such as the LZ8, *Hindenberg* and *Graf Zeppelin* would dwarf present day airliners such as Concorde, although they carried fewer passengers.

head wind

turbulent winds

mountains

LZ8 173 metres long

Graf Zeppelin 236 metres long

Hindenburg 245 metres long

Concorde 64 metres long

warning at all, the *Graf Zeppelin* ran into a severe storm. Eckener was thrown from his position in the control cabin as all around him pieces of equipment flew through the air. They survived the buffeting, however, and the veteran airship commander was soon back in control. An inspection of the zeppelin revealed a tear in the canvas of one of the rear fins, which could jam the elevator if left unattended. With speed reduced, a work party, including Eckener's son Knut, climbed out on to the fin and carried out emergency repairs. Meanwhile, as a precaution, Eckener sent a wireless message asking the US navy for assistance. The radio then went silent

for a time as the airship was travelling too slowly to drive the air-driven electricity generator, so the call for help seemed very dramatic and made front page headlines in American newspapers. Some people thought the *Graf Zeppelin* had crashed, so when she finally appeared unharmed over New York, a great crowd gathered to welcome the airship and her crew.

Graf Zeppelin in the public eye

Eckener realized on this trip that with winds of 100 to 130 kph, any regular North Atlantic service would require a faster airship than *Graf Zeppelin*, but he could not see any way of getting

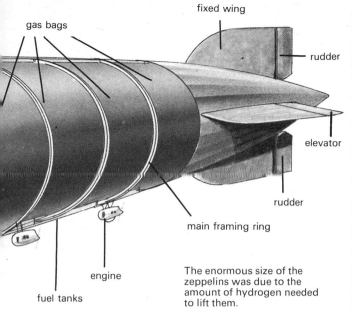

gas bags

fixed wing

rudder

elevator

rudder

main framing ring

engine

fuel tanks

The enormous size of the zeppelins was due to the amount of hydrogen needed to lift them.

Below: The airships were always at risk in strong winds. L20 was wrecked after taking shelter in a Norwegian fjord in 1916.

immediate financial support for such a project. He realized that he must keep *Graf Zeppelin* in the public eye to foster confidence in the airship, and so he planned a series of attention-winning voyages.

First he invited prominent influential businessmen and politicians on a flight around the Mediterranean. The whole trip, from the German snow to the sun and back, took only 80 hours and won over to the airship's cause some of the most important men in Germany.

Eckener was soon planning an even more impressive voyage. He intended to take the *Graf Zeppelin* and a full load of passengers on a round-the-world trip with only three stops en route. The American millionaire William Randolph Hearst sponsored the trip on condition it started and finished in New York. Accordingly, Eckener took the *Graf Zeppelin* across the Atlantic in August 1929 and landed safely at Lakehurst.

The trip started on 9 August with the 55-hour voyage back to Friedrichshafen where more passengers were being picked up, before setting out across Russia for the next stop in Tokyo, Japan. As they passed north of Moscow, the terrain 1,000 metres below grew more rugged, and there were few signs of human habitation. At the eastern edge of the Siberian plateau the Stanovoi Mountains rise to 2,500 metres. Eckener was following a valley, but the whole area was poorly charted and as the *Graf Zeppelin* moved forward, the ground below suddenly seemed to rise to meet them. Summoning all his skill Eckener guided his zeppelin over the mountain crest with only 30 metres to spare.

They then flew over the Sea of Okhotsk, and on 19 August the *Graf Zeppelin* touched down outside Tokyo. The airship still had enough fuel on board to reach Los Angeles non-stop, but Eckener, who had already upset the Russians by not flying over Moscow, decided that it might seriously affect his company's relations with the Japanese if he bypassed Tokyo.

Insufficient gas

One week later, the *Graf Zeppelin* arrived in Los Angeles, having left Tokyo just 80 hours earlier. As the airship lay in the Californian sunshine, the hydrogen gas expanded and was valved off automatically to prevent a pressure build-up. So when Eckener came to take off there was insufficient gas to raise the zeppelin. With weight reduced to a minimum the *Graf Zeppelin* just managed to rise a few metres into the air. Eckener eased the airship forward, trying to use his forward speed to gain height. They were travelling fairly quickly when Eckener saw power lines ahead. He left evasive manoeuvres to the last minute then ordered, 'full nose-up on the controls'. With the nose high in the air, the tail was left dragging almost along the ground towards the power cables. Then Eckener ordered 'full nose-down'. The tail came up and the 230-metre long airship porpoised neatly over the obstacle to safety. A long slow climb took the zeppelin to cruising height, and after a relatively uneventful journey they reached Lakehurst where the usual large and enthusiastic crowd of people were waiting to greet them.

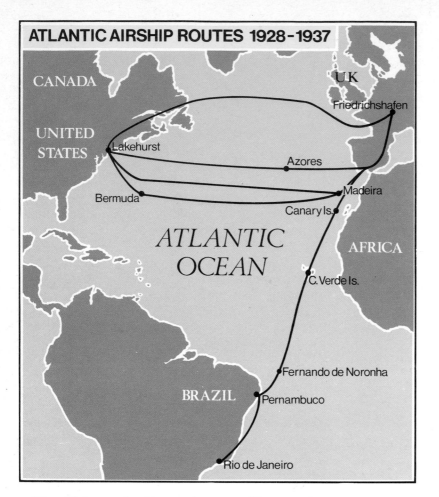

ATLANTIC AIRSHIP ROUTES 1928-1937

CANADA

UK

Friedrichshafen

UNITED STATES

Lakehurst

Azores

Madeira

Bermuda

Canary Is.

ATLANTIC OCEAN

AFRICA

C. Verde Is.

Fernando de Noronha

BRAZIL

Pernambuco

Rio de Janeiro

The *Hindenberg* crash was a great disaster, but 62 of the 97 people aboard survived.

The flight excited great interest. To sustain that interest, Eckener pushed himself and the *Graf Zeppelin* hard. In 1930 he took the airship to South America, and a survey of the Arctic followed the next year. In 1933 regular passenger services to South America were started.

The Hindenburg

The success of the *Graf Zeppelin* and the prestige that Germany gained from the flights Eckener made, encouraged the new German National Socialist government under Adolf Hitler to finance the construction of a new airship which was to be larger and faster than the *Graf Zeppelin*. At the same time, Eckener was removed from the post of Flight Operations Director and made chairman of the board. Eckener opposed the Nazis and would not allow their swastika symbol to be painted on the *Graf Zeppelin*. He was also immensely popular and was a possible candidate for Chancellor of Germany, a position which Hitler himself coveted. 'Promoting' Eckener to the board moved him out of the limelight and also gave the government more control of the Zeppelin Company.

The new airship, named *Hindenburg*, was the most luxurious flying machine ever built. She carried 50 passengers and was designed to use helium gas which was safer than flammable hydrogen. The USA refused to export helium to Germany, however, and as that was the only source, hydrogen had to be used.

For a year the *Hindenburg* operated passenger services to New York. Then, on 6 May 1937, while approaching Lakehurst to land, a spark ignited some leaking hydrogen. Within moments the airship was ablaze from end to end. Miraculously 62 of the 97 people aboard escaped, but the disaster marked the end of the airship.

Eckener was a member of the board of inquiry into the accident, and afterwards he tried to save the Zeppelin Company, which had already built a sister to the *Hindenburg*, called *Graf Zeppelin II*. Although this zeppelin made some demonstration flights, the public had lost faith in the airship, and no more scheduled services were operated. At the outbreak of the Second World War the remaining zeppelins were broken up and the scrap aluminium was turned into aeroplanes. Eckener lived in quiet retirement until his death in 1954.

Peter Reeves

An English pilot in the
Second World War, 1940

15 September 1940

Dear Philip,

I am writing from an airfield 'somewhere in the south of England' as the censor will only allow us to say. I joined the squadron only last month, after completing my training, the worst part of which was definitely the first two weeks at the Initial Training Wing [ITW]. When you leave Oxford you may find that the only reason for ITW's existence is to bash some 'military discipline' into such University Air Squadron [UAS] types as ourselves.

The American-built Harvard was a popular RAF trainer.

We soon moved on to the Flying Training School, flying Harvards. The Harvard was a real shock after the Tiger Moth at UAS, as it has a retractable undercarriage, flaps and variable pitch propeller. At least it is a two-seater, so we could have some dual instruction before flying solo. This is not the case with the Spitfire, as no one has yet got round to designing a two-seat version. The best preparation they can offer for flying the 'Spit' is a few dual circuits in a Miles Master which in some way resembles it. Then you are left to yourself with the Spitfire.

It wasn't until I actually sat in a Spitfire that I had any idea of the problems involved even when still on the ground. The forward view is almost non-existent because of the massive Merlin engine ahead. When taxiing you have to weave hard from side to side to see ahead at all. If the engine is kept running for too long on the ground it overheats, as the radiators are blocked by the undercarriage legs, and even when the aircraft is airborne the problems are not over. To retract the undercarriage you take your left

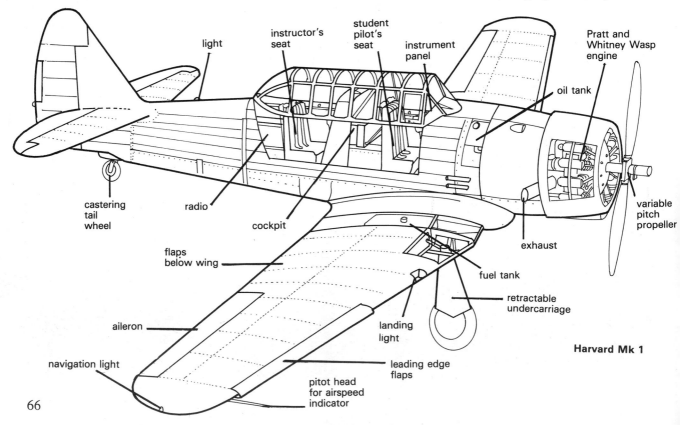

light — instructor's seat — student pilot's seat — instrument panel — Pratt and Whitney Wasp engine — oil tank — castering tail wheel — radio — cockpit — variable pitch propeller — flaps below wing — exhaust — fuel tank — retractable undercarriage — aileron — landing light — navigation light — leading edge flaps — pitot head for airspeed indicator

Harvard Mk 1

Key: 1. Control column 2. Gun button 3. Flight instruments 4. Engine instruments 5. Compass 6. Undercarriage selector lever 7. Undercarriage hand pump 8. Undercarriage indicator 9 Rudder bar 10. Flap lever

The cockpit of a Spitfire

hand off the throttle, change hands on the control column then wind up the wheels with the right hand. Most of the squadron come out to watch a new pilot's first Spitfire take-off. If you don't tighten the nut on the throttle in the fully open position it vibrates shut, leaving you with an aeroplane still at a very low altitude, with drag from the undercarriage, and with no power. It flies like a brick! So far, this squadron has lost as many aircraft in take-off and landing accidents as the Germans have shot down.

We had a visit from a flight of German bombers last week. They didn't damage the air-field much, but one bomb landed among three Spitfires which were just taking off. Two of them ended up flat on their backs and their pilots walked away unhurt. The third simply dis-appeared from sight, and we were getting quite concerned until the pilot walked in the front gate of the airfield some 4 hours later. It turned out that his aircraft had cartwheeled through the air for quite some way, ending up on the other side of the boundary hedge. After releasing himself from the wreck, the poor bloke had to walk a long way around the airfield perimeter before he could get back in. The control room was also hit, but by the next morning the plotters had set up their tables and telephone lines in the local butcher's shop and were directing the squadrons as usual.

We spend most of the day lying in the sun beside the aircraft at dispersal, waiting for the call to come through for the squadron to scramble. To an outsider it would look very strange. One moment we are all sitting on the grass reading, talking or playing cards. The next moment a telephone rings and we are all running

Below: The Spitfire, designed by RJ Mitchell, was produced throughout the Second World War. Over 20,000 were built.

like fury for the aeroplanes. We usually keep on our Mae West lifejackets, so we just snatch up our helmets and parachutes before strapping in. The fitter tightens our harness while we plug in the R/T [Radio Telephony] and oxygen leads. Within minutes the squadron is in the air, climbing hard on full power. The golden rule is to get above the opponent, so normally we climb away from the incoming Germans until we are high enough to engage them from a good position.

Most of the pre-war ideas we were taught in the UAS have been thrown away by the front-line squadrons. I remember seeing the Empire Air Day displays where the Gloster Gladiators flew in formation with their wing tips joined together with short cables. We soon found out that tight formations like that are no use in modern air combat and now, when the fighting starts, we work in pairs, with one man covering the other's tail. The Spitfire has an edge on the main German fighter, the Bf109. It turns very much tighter, and is just as fast, but the poor old Hurricane squadrons take a bit of a pasting sometimes, as they are considerably slower.

We all had rather a field day when the Italians came over. They had some twin-engined bombers and biplane fighters, which I am told were Fiat CR.42s. The bombers were easy to shoot down, although their crews were surprisingly brave, and tried to press home the attack though totally outnumbered and outperformed. The fighters were a different matter, though they were much slower than the Spitfire. The biplanes could turn on a sixpence so it was almost impossible to aim the guns at them for long enough to shoot them down. The Germans were notable by their absence so I don't think they have too much confidence in the Italians.

We have quite a few nationalities in the squadron. The most impressive, and to the Germans possibly the most terrifying, are two Poles who

Below: The Italian Air Force's outdated aircraft, such as the Fiat CR.42, were no match for the Spitfires and Hurricanes of the RAF.

Left: Important work was done by the people in the plotting room, tracking enemy aircraft and instructing defending squadrons to 'scramble'.

Below: Pilots sat around in full flying gear waiting for the call to 'scramble', when they would rush for their aircraft.

Above: The close-formation flying of these Gladiators, and the complex manoeuvres which the RAF practised before the Second World War were found to be useless in the fast-moving dogfights of the Battle of Britain.

flew their aircraft to RAF bases when the Polish Air Force collapsed. They are good fellows, but in the heat of battle they get a bit excited and scream at each other in Polish over the R/T. The next moment the pair of them will go chasing away after some poor German who usually doesn't know what's hit him. They are impossible to control at such times, though the Commanding Officer of another squadron manages to discipline his Poles by banning them from flying next day if they disobey orders.

Until last week we had an American here who had volunteered to join the RAF because he felt that somebody in America had to do something to help. He has now been posted to a new squadron nicknamed 'Eagle Squadron' which is composed totally of Americans. The last of our foreigners is a Frenchman who flies with the Cross of Lorraine, the sign of the Free French, on his aeroplane. I have heard that there are even some Germans fighting for the RAF. They are

Jewish refugees who left Germany before the war. The British use them mainly in intelligence work because of their knowledge of Germany. When they joined up they were given new identities as Britons for fear that if they were ever captured, the Germans would treat them as traitors.

I had quite a strange experience the last time I flew. We had scrambled to intercept some inbound German aircraft, and our controller gave us our instructions as usual: 'Vector 180, Bandits 15 at Angels 120.' [Make your compass heading 180°, target 15 aircraft at 12,000 feet/3,500 metres.] Then suddenly we heard a German voice in our earphones. Coincidentally, the Germans were using the same radio channel, and for some minutes we hurled insults at each other in various languages!

Jimmy Turpin, whom you may remember from Oxford as he was in the same college as you, had a near-miraculous escape last week. He made the mistake of following a damaged 109 out over the Channel, where he was bounced by another three Germans. He put one of them down but

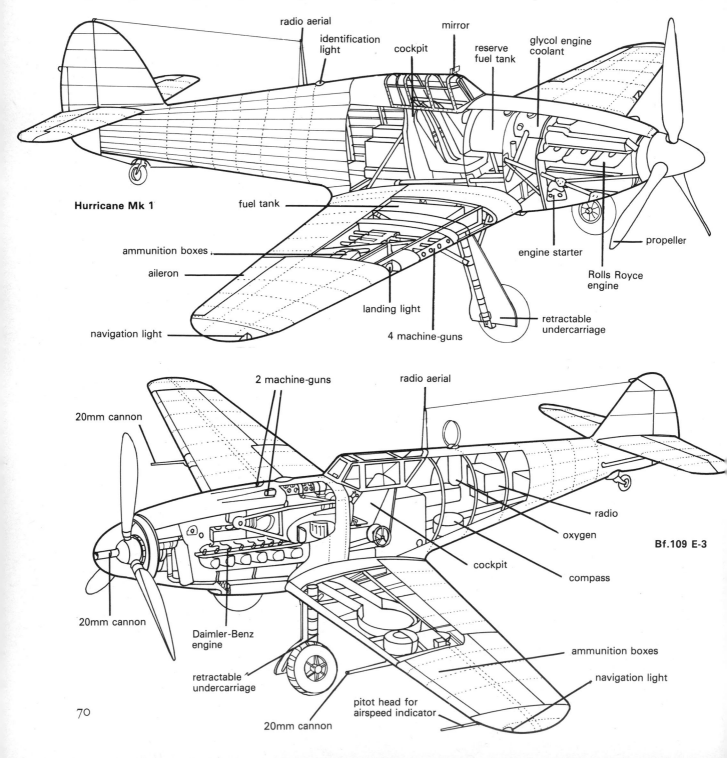

Hurricane Mk 1

radio aerial
identification light
cockpit
mirror
reserve fuel tank
glycol engine coolant
propeller
engine starter
Rolls Royce engine
retractable undercarriage
fuel tank
ammunition boxes
aileron
navigation light
landing light
4 machine-guns

Bf.109 E-3

2 machine-guns
radio aerial
20mm cannon
radio
oxygen
cockpit
compass
20mm cannon
Daimler-Benz engine
ammunition boxes
navigation light
retractable undercarriage
20mm cannon
pitot head for airspeed indicator

was himself shot up. A Hurricane pilot who was nearby said that Jimmy's Spitfire caught fire and entered a spin at about 9,000 feet [2,800 metres]. Jimmy was unconscious but was thrown clear as the aircraft twisted down. When he came to, he pulled his ripcord and parachuted down to a safe but wet landing in the Channel. The Hurricane pilot radioed his position and stayed there until an air–sea rescue launch picked him up. Jimmy was rather badly burned, but it's amazing what the surgeons can do now. They certainly get plenty of practice as many of our aircraft don't yet have self-sealing tanks, so they often catch fire if a German puts shells through the tanks.

Many of the seriously burned pilots have shown amazing courage, and some have returned to flying or to ground jobs as controllers. The top surgeon in the burns unit is a fellow by the name of McIndoe, and the aircrew who have been

Below: Pilots autographed a blackboard in a bar near Biggin Hill airfield.

treated by him call themselves 'The Guinea Pig Club'. I'm sure Jimmy Turpin could not be in better hands.

I myself had to bale out soon after joining the squadron. The engine of my kite had taken a bit of a pasting during a scrap just over Dover. As I was returning to base the temperature started to rise and I could see the glycol liquid, used to cool the engine, leaking back along the fuselage. I had opened the canopy, ready to jump if necessary but hoping to get her down in one piece, when, with a great bang, the engine seized and oil covered the windscreen. Even if there had been any open space to put her down in, I could see nothing for the coating of oil, so I simply undid the straps, rolled her on her back and dropped out. It was quite peaceful drifting down under a great white parachute, but once I had landed on the ground it was a different story. I first had to convince the local Home Guardsman that I was not a German parachutist intent on capturing Britain alone, with my bare hands. Then I faced the problem of returning to the airfield. I took a train into London, then, as there was an air raid in progress, I could not find a taxi. I was preparing to walk across the city to catch another train back here when a friendly ambulance driver took pity on me and gave me a lift. That evening I was back in the air again, flying a new aircraft which had just been delivered.

The attitude of the local people here has changed amazingly over the past few months. At the time of the evacuation of Dunkirk in June, very few of the soldiers had ever seen an RAF aircraft, and very few German aircraft were found on this side of the Channel. Many British people felt that the RAF was not pulling its weight, and the boys who have been in the squadron since the early days say that they were quite often insulted in the street by some old girl who thought they should be doing some 'real' fighting. That's all changed now, and we could become quite swell-headed by the attention we receive. At Biggin Hill the local pub has a blackboard in the bar where every pilot, no matter how junior, signs his name. The terrifying thing is how few of those pilots are still with us. I only hope that once we finish this mess, the people will remember those boys as more than a few names on a blackboard.

I hope it won't be too long before you get the chance to join a squadron. Till then – happy landings!

Yours,

Charles Yeager

The first supersonic flight, 1947

Captain Charles 'Chuck' Yeager was the first man to fly faster than sound, piloting the Bell X-1 on 14 October 1947. His achievement followed much research in Britain, Germany and the USA into the problems caused by exceeding the speed of sound. That speed is called Mach 1 after the nineteenth-century Austrian physicist, Ernst Mach, who did a great deal of the basic research. Similarly, speeds lower than that of sound are described as decimal parts, for instance, Mach 0.8.

Such World War Two aircraft as the Spitfire and the P51 Mustang could achieve high subsonic speeds in a dive, but they then became practically uncontrollable. Several pilots lost their lives after encountering such problems, including Geoffrey de Havilland Junior who died in 1946 when flying a de Havilland DH.108 designed by his father's company. The resulting publicity created the popular image of the 'sound barrier'. In Britain, the development of the Miles M.52 supersonic research aircraft was stopped after it was decided that manned flight at those speeds was too dangerous.

In the USA, however, the National Advisory Committee for Aeronautics (NACA) continued their research programme and turned to the Bell Aircraft Corporation for a suitable aircraft. To find a pilot the US Air Force (USAF) looked to

The X-1 was painted bright orange to make recognition and observation easier.

their Fighter Test Section at Wright Patterson Air Force Base in Dayton, Ohio. The man they chose was a 24-year-old West Virginian named Charles Yeager. He was an experienced pilot who had flown fighters over Europe during the Second World War. Early in 1944, only a few months after his arrival in Europe, he was shot down over France, but after baling out he managed to avoid capture and made his way back to Britain via Spain. He returned to flying duties, and by the time he went back to the USA he had shot down twelve enemy aircraft and been awarded several medals. After completing an instructors' course in America, he was posted to the Fighter Test Section and from there, through a rigorous selection process, he found his way on to the NACA supersonic project in 1947.

The Bell X-1

By that time the Bell Corporation had designed and flown the X-1, the aircraft which NACA had commissioned. It carried one pilot and was powered by a Reaction Motors rocket engine. This engine comprised four separate chambers and the only control the pilot had over speed was the number of chambers he ignited – two, three or all four.

Most accidents which happened at near supersonic speeds at that time, were caused by the aircraft breaking up, so Bell built the X-1 to withstand 18g, that is 18 times the force of

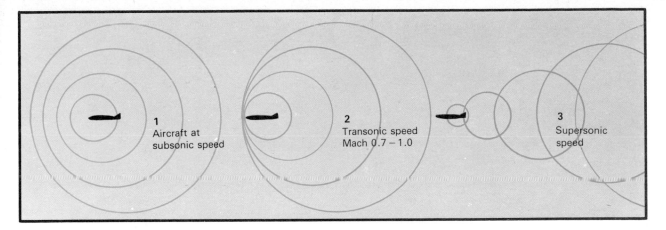

1 Aircraft at subsonic speed

2 Transonic speed Mach 0.7 – 1.0

3 Supersonic speed

How speed records in the air became faster

Date	kph/mph	Pilot	Aircraft
1909	74/46	Blériot	Blériot monoplane
1911	120/74	Nieuport	Nieuport monoplane
1913	204/127	Prévost	Deperdussin monoplane
1920	309/192	de Romanet	Spad biplane
1923	411/255	Brown	Curtiss HS D-12
1928	513/319	de Bernardi	Macchi M-52
1931	655/407	Stainforth	Supermarine S6B
1939	755/469	Wendel	Messerschmitt Bf 109R
1945	976/606	Wilson	Gloster Meteor F4
1947	1078/670	Yeager	Bell X-1*
1953	1152/716	Barnes	F-86D Sabre
1956	1821/1132	Twiss	Fairey Delta 2
1959	2387/1484	Mosolov	Mikoyan E-66
1962	2681/1666	Mosolov	Mikoyan E-166
1967	7297/4534	Knight	Bell X-15 A-2*
1976	3529/2193	Joerz and Morgan	Lockheed SR-71A

*The Bell X-1 and X-15 did not take off from the Earth under their own power.

Below: The Bell X-1 was designed to use a new design of turbo-rocket, but as this engine was not completed quickly enough the Reaction Motors rocket was fitted. The fuels used were liquid oxygen and alcohol, which were fed under pressure into the chambers of the rocket. The maximum power available was 26·7 kilonewtons, less than 1/30th of that of a Boeing 747, and the 2730 litres of fuel lasted less than three minutes, a fuel consumption of approximately 56 litres per kilometre.

Above: Approaching Mach 1·0, a shock wave builds up ahead of the aircraft. At supersonic speeds the wave is left behind as sonic booms.

Reaction Motors rocket

73

gravity. To make the aircraft lighter it did not carry enough fuel for the climb and was to be air-launched from beneath a converted B-29 Superfortress. By the time the X-1, serial number 6062, was handed over to the Air Force it had been launched several times in gliding trials to check for correct separation from the mother ship. Once the engine had been fitted, the X-1 had been flown up to Mach 0.8 by Bell's own test pilots. Beyond Mach 0.8 the behaviour of the aircraft was impossible to predict, and it was this transonic area which Chuck Yeager had been selected to investigate.

In August 1947 Yeager made his first flight in the X-1, named *Glamorous Glennis* after his wife. The craft was launched without any fuel from the B-29 at about 8,500 metres and glided all the way down to a safe landing on the dried-up salt lake that was used as a runway. The reason for this flight was to let the pilot familiarize himself with the aircraft, especially its approach and

Above: The X-1 being prepared for flight. The white marks are ice caused by the supercooled liquid nitrogen.

landing characteristics. The X-1 always glided down to land, which alone called for special skill. It also landed at very high speeds – around 325 kph – so the dangers and difficulties were multiplied. Yeager made three unpowered flights before he was satisfied.

Powered flights

On the first flight using the engine, Yeager lit only three of the rocket chambers, and after parting from the mother ship he climbed rapidly to 12,000 metres, and accelerated to Mach 0.87 before cutting the motor and gliding down to a safe landing. One compartment of the X-1 was packed with instruments which measured all the forces affecting the aircraft and this information was recorded for analysis on the ground after the flight. The most important details were transmitted back to earth during the flight by a radio

The Bell X-1 had the smallest airframe in which the pilot, fuel and engine could be accommodated. No space was wasted.

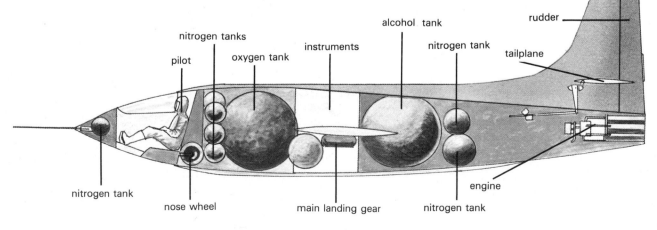

Above: The combination of a B-29 bomber carrying the X-1 was used for most of the test flights.

link, and there was also a camera in the cockpit to photograph the instrument panel.

The research team had decided to explore the area up to Mach 1 gradually, so the next flight was made to Mach 0.89, and the third one to Mach 0.91. On each of these flights Yeager found that control difficulties increased. Later research showed that a supersonic shock wave formed on the wing before the aircraft reached Mach 1. This wave interfered with the airflow over the wing, causing severe vibration. At the same time it reduced the effectiveness of the controls, making it very difficult to recover the aircraft from manoeuvres such as a steep dive.

On the fourth flight Yeager found that because of the shock wave, the elevator, the surface which controlled the vertical movement of the aeroplane, became almost useless at about Mach 0.94. He managed to manoeuvre the aircraft by moving the whole tailplane, instead of just the elevator surfaces. This technique produced the later 'all-flying tailplane' used on most modern jets.

Flying at the speed of sound

On 14 October 1947, Yeager strapped himself into the X-1 suspended below the B-29, and carefully checked the aircraft's systems. The X-1 carried bottles of compressed nitrogen which was used to pressurize the fuel tanks, to lower the flaps and undercarriage and to power the gyros of the flight instruments. Yeager therefore gave special attention to the nitrogen system. He also checked the fuel system, a combination of liquid oxygen and alcohol carried in separate fuselage tanks. Rocket fuels can be dangerous, and the second X-1 later had to be jettisoned after it caught fire in the bomb bay of its mother ship. Luckily, this happened before the pilot got in.

On this occasion, however, all was well. Yeager gave the signal, and the X-1 dropped away from

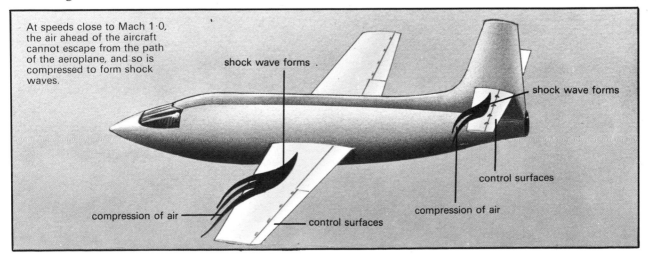

At speeds close to Mach 1·0, the air ahead of the aircraft cannot escape from the path of the aeroplane, and so is compressed to form shock waves.

shock wave forms

shock wave forms

compression of air

control surfaces

control surfaces

compression of air

beneath the Superfortress. At 8,500 metres Yeager ignited the four rocket chambers, and the X-1, painted bright orange for easier observation from the ground, began to climb on its 2·5 minutes' worth of fuel. As he accelerated he again experienced the severe shaking and control problems until, at 12,000 metres, with the Machmeter indicating Mach 1.015 (at that height around 1,078 kph), he entered the smoothness of supersonic flight. Yeager cut the engine for the flight back to earth. The flight opened the way to a new era in air travel – the supersonic age. The Con-corde carries 100 passengers in shirt-sleeve comfort at Mach 2 and at 17,000 metres.

Yeager made further flights in the X-1, eventually reaching Mach 1.5, but his last X-1 flight, though subsonic, was possibly the most dangerous of all, as it involved a conventional take-off from a runway instead of the normal air launch. Despite fears of a power failure or loss of control, Yeager made the flight successfully, and reached 7,000 metres before the limited supply of fuel ran out. He also made several flights in a new version of the X-1 called the

The flight path of the Bell X-1

12,000 metres

10,500 metres

separation from
B.29 Superfortress

8,500 metres

climb and
acceleration

rocket ignition

In the Bell X-1 Yeager travelled at speeds then unknown to man.

Above: A photograph of the X-1 and its B-29 motherplane, taken by Chuck Yeager on the day of the first supersonic flight.

X-1A, and in 1953, flying this aircraft, he reached Mach 2.5, about 2,640 kph.

For his work in extending the boundaries of flight, Yeager received many awards and medals, including the Distinguished Service Medal from the USAF. He eventually returned to his normal air force duties with the USAF in Germany. The Bell X-1 was presented to the Smithsonian Institute in Washington DC, where it is displayed alongside the first powered aircraft, the Wright brothers' *Flyer*, which had made its first flight less than 50 years earlier.

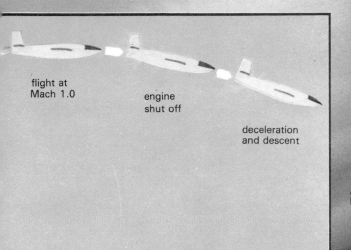

flight at
Mach 1.0

engine
shut off

deceleration
and descent

Above: Yeager, who qualified for the job of piloting the X-1 because of his experience as a combat airman and test pilot

John Burns

A flying doctor in Australia, 1968

The Australian outback is a dried-up inland sea containing immense salt lakes and occasional rock outcrops. The few rivers in the area flood every two or three years and turn the land into a muddy, impassable nightmare. For the sick and injured there is little hope of help reaching them by road or rail. Since its formation in 1927, the Royal Flying Doctor Service has answered the calls for assistance of the stockmen, miners and other settlers, carrying a doctor to them by air.

When John Burns finished his medical training in 1968 at Guy's Hospital in London, he was offered a permanent post on the hospital staff. The salary was very good, and the prospects for a young doctor were promising, but he felt homesick for his native Australia, and also felt a need to do more than assist the consultants who controlled the patients' treatment. After much consideration he travelled back to Australia and visited a colleague at a large Sydney hospital to find out about positions there. He soon realized that he would not be happy working in a hospital where the scope for individual initiative was limited, and when a friend suggested that the Royal Flying Doctor Service might be more suitable, John was very interested.

The de Havilland Dragon was used by the Flying Doctor Service in the 1930s. It had good short landing capabilities and could operate from rough farm fields.

He soon found that the service had come a long way since 1927. It had been founded by a missionary named John Flynn, and in the early days it had one doctor and chartered an aircraft from a developing airline called Queensland and Northern Territory Air Services, now known as QANTAS. Before that time there had been few doctors in the area of north west Australia, which the new service covered. Those doctors who were available on the coast, in places like Darwin, were a long way from the small inland mining and farming communities and were not always of the highest standard. One, who was a political refugee from Russia, spoke no English and his daughter had to interpret for him.

The chance of successful treatment

The DH.50 aircraft used by the flying doctors in the late 20s were fitted with a stretcher and had a special soft undercarriage to avoid bumping the patient. The Flying Doctor Service brought the chance of successful treatment to the people of isolated areas, at a time when influenza could kill because the correct drugs were not available, and where there was no one skilled in using them. Now the service had its own fleet of 27 aircraft, many of them twin-engined, and it was run almost like an airline, with professional pilots and its own engineering staff.

John discovered that he would not be paid a great deal as the service did not charge its patients for treatment, and existed on charitable contributions and a subsidy from the state government. He felt that as he had no family responsibilities he did not need much money, and in any case, living and working in the outback he would have little opportunity to spend it. So, he took an Ansett Airlines flight to Alice Springs.

Alice Springs is in the Northern Territory, one of the most rugged areas of Australia, and John soon found he was going to be very busy. At night there was an alarm system to waken the radio operator and the doctor, should there be an emergency radio call. The first night he was there, John was wakened twice. The first time he prescribed penicillin over the radio, for a farmhand who had an infected cut in his leg. Years before, the medical services' doctors devised a first aid kit containing most of the emergency supplies that a small community might require. Each item in the kit was numbered and carried brief instructions for use. The doctor simply gave the correct numbers over the radio, and most minor problems could be taken care of.

The second call was more serious. A small mining community near Barrow Creek, 300 kilometres north of Alice Springs, was suffering from a suspected outbreak of typhoid and one miner had died. At first light, John met his pilot at the local airstrip. Gordon Thompson was an ex-Royal Australian Air Force pilot who had joined the Royal Flying Doctor Service instead of working for a large international airline like QANTAS. He was pilot, navigator and engineer rolled into one, and when away from base it was his responsibility to refuel the aircraft, often manhandling 25-litre drums of fuel, and to make emergency repairs.

The aircraft they were to use was a twin-engined Beechcraft Baron. It could carry six people and its 265 horsepower engines gave it a top speed of 320 kph. The cabin had been converted to carry a stretcher and an attendant. On this occasion a nurse from the State hospital accompanied John and Gordon and she brought the serum with which they would inoculate the stricken townspeople.

The control tower gave the Baron immediate take-off clearance and they were soon heading north, following the main highway towards Barrow Creek.

Hazardous flights

The flights that the doctors had to take were often hazardous. Although the aircraft carried modern radio navigation aids, and the pilots were fully qualified to fly only on instruments, most of the flying doctors' missions took place in the backward areas of Australia where there were few radio facilities on the ground. Fortunately most of the flying was in good weather, though occasional sandstorms could create difficulties. In one case, a pilot flew for several kilometres only a few metres above a fence which was the only object he could see through the swirling sand. Eventually, the fence led him to his destination where he landed safely. Landings could be dangerous too, as the airstrips were primitive and the weather could change suddenly. Night landings were

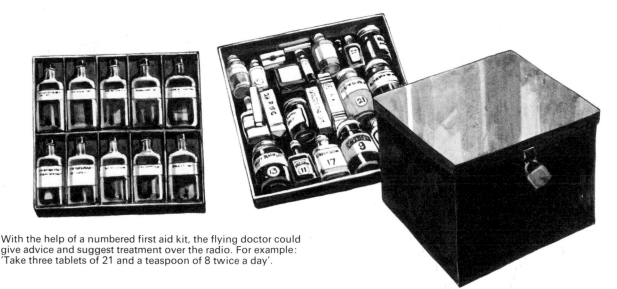

With the help of a numbered first aid kit, the flying doctor could give advice and suggest treatment over the radio. For example: 'Take three tablets of 21 and a teaspoon of 8 twice a day'.

Most flying doctor aircraft
carry a nurse to administer
emergency treatment in flight
and to restrain struggling
patients.

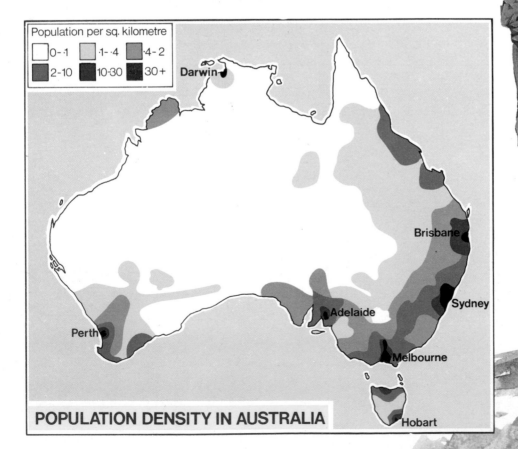

Population per sq. kilometre

0-·1 ·1-·4 ·4-2
2-10 10-30 30+

Darwin

Brisbane

Adelaide

Perth

Sydney

Melbourne

Hobart

POPULATION DENSITY IN AUSTRALIA

Above: The aircraft used by the service must be rugged and reliable for flights over the Australian outback.

difficult and only performed in emergencies as the only lighting normally available was the headlamps of cars shining along the runway. Landing areas were always checked from the ground before being approved for use, as ruts or holes could wreck the aeroplane. Some of the long grasses which grew in the wet areas could hide fallen trees which would remove a plane's undercarriage. Any aircraft which became bogged down in sand or mud could be stuck for days and many men would be required to move it. In some instances, the pilot was forced to land the doctor some distance from the shack where his patient lay. The flying doctor then faced a long walk through difficult terrain, and eventually he might have to perform a difficult operation.

John and his crew landed safely after a good flight, close to the nameless collection of shacks which had called for help only hours earlier. Very soon the inoculation programme was under way, and once this was completed John made some

The flying doctor's duties include routine inoculation programmes as well as emergency treatment.

tests and took a few samples from which the laboratory could establish if this outbreak really was typhoid. By midday he was back in Alice Springs for a session of radio consultations.

Advice over the radio

These sessions took place three times a week. Any of his patients who had medical problems could call the flying doctor on the radio and ask for his advice. The radios were the latest technology in long-range transmitters which had a range of several thousand kilometres. The original flying doctor network was built around the radio transmitter designed by Alfred Traeger. The service's founder, John Flynn, asked Traeger to design a radio with which a layman without any electrical power could transmit over long distances. He produced an ingenious design powered by pedals. The operator sat at a keyboard like a typewriter's and 'typed' out his message while pedalling to produce power. When he, or she, typed the letter A the radio transmitted ·- (dot, dash), the morse letter A.

Once 'voice' radios were introduced, the network developed uses other than purely medical ones. The schools of the air were introduced to help educate children in isolated areas where the only other schooling came from a correspondence course.

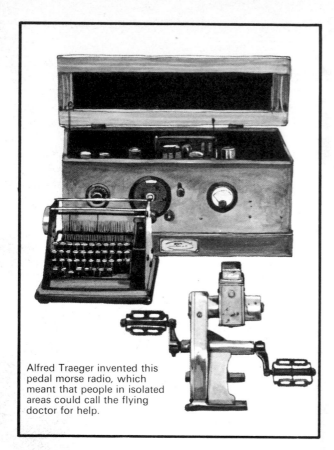

Alfred Traeger invented this pedal morse radio, which meant that people in isolated areas could call the flying doctor for help.

Below: The service relied on the use of radio to call for help, and to get advice before the doctor arrived.

Occasionally, during the early days of the service, the flying doctors had to deal with victims of fights among the Aborigines living in the remote areas.

Many of the early doctors flew the aircraft themselves and this led to problems on several occasions when a delirious patient became violent in midair. Sometimes the doctor was reduced to knocking the patient unconscious, though this was inadvisable if the patient was already suffering from a head injury! In some cases when they were dealing with the Aborigines the doctors had to overcome superstition and myth before they could begin treatment. Tribal fights were common and one flying doctor who was called to treat a wounded woman found that the spear which was still embedded in her chest was so long that the poor woman would not fit in the aeroplane. The doctor cut the ends off the spear and took the woman to hospital where the rest of the weapon was removed.

John soon settled to the busy and unpredictable life of a flying doctor. He was very relieved when the typhoid tests the laboratory ran proved negative, but he was soon occupied with other work. Sometimes he simply gave pain-killing drugs to his patients, and then accompanied them in the aircraft to hospital, but on other occasions he had to operate immediately and in difficult conditions. John found satisfaction, however, in belonging to a service that was using the skills and technology of the twentieth century to help people who were living in some of the most difficult conditions in the civilized world.

Glen Stewart

A pilot of a Space Shuttle Orbiter, 1985

Glen Stewart sat in the command pilot's position on Orbiter 103 *Discovery*, listening to the countdown of the controller who occupied the firing room a short distance from the Kennedy Space Centre's launch complex 39A. This would be Stewart's third and last Shuttle trip into space as he was retiring to a desk job on his return. As the chatter of the specialists checking the spacecraft systems continued, he mused on the twenty years he had spent as an astronaut. When he had joined the Gemini programme in 1965 the word 'astronaut' was still new, and in the eyes of the public and the press, the young men who made the first orbits of the Earth were little short of supermen. Now, much of that had changed and the whole business of space travel had become more of an everyday event, and sometimes seemed almost monotonous.

The countdown reached the stage where the pilots began their pre-ignition checks. Stewart gave his full concentration to the actions and responses demanded of him by the check list read out by his young co-pilot, Ken Greene. Greene was a product of NASA's (the National Aeronautical and Space Administration's) latest training programme. The programme was aimed at producing sufficient astronauts for the planned 45 Shuttle launches every year. To his commander, Greene was an example of the changes in the space programme. He was the result of a production line system which in four years had trained 70 men and women for Shuttle operations. Then Glen decided it wasn't the people who had changed so much – it was the job itself. He had flown on the Gemini missions in orbit round the Earth in the sixties, and on the Apollo Moon missions which culminated in 1969 with Neil Armstrong's historic Moon landing. By the luck of the draw, Stewart himself had never landed on the Moon, but nevertheless, in those days every mission pioneered a new step forward in space travel. Now that had gone, and each flight seemed much like the last to the pilots. The pioneering had passed to the scientists who sat as passengers until *Discovery* reached orbit.

door   Spacelab

The Spacelab project is a joint European Space Agency and NASA project which will provide facilities for four scientists to conduct research and experiments in a laboratory moving at 25,000 kph under weightless conditions, 110 kilometres above the Earth.

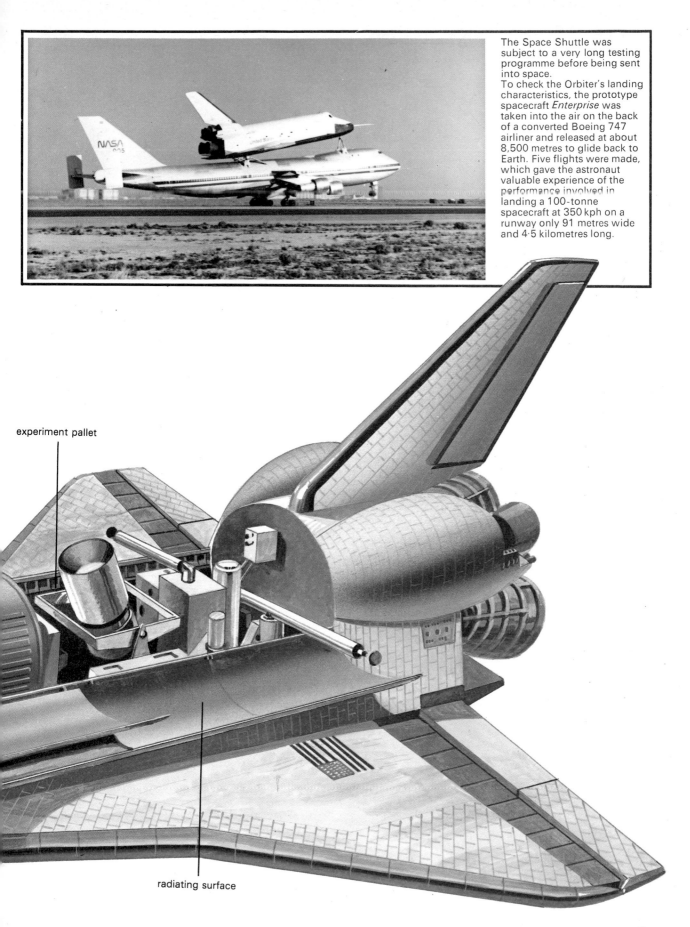

The Space Shuttle was subject to a very long testing programme before being sent into space.
To check the Orbiter's landing characteristics, the prototype spacecraft *Enterprise* was taken into the air on the back of a converted Boeing 747 airliner and released at about 8,500 metres to glide back to Earth. Five flights were made, which gave the astronaut valuable experience of the performance involved in landing a 100-tonne spacecraft at 350 kph on a runway only 91 metres wide and 4·5 kilometres long.

experiment pallet

radiating surface

The specialist on this mission, Gordon Fulwell, was also a veteran of the Apollo missions, but his scientific background gave him the interest in continued space travel which Stewart found he was now losing. Below, in the living quarters, were the three scientists who were responsible for the running of the experiments in Spacelab which occupied the Orbiter's cargo bay. Spacelab was a project between America and Europe which gave scientists the chance to carry out experiments in the unique conditions of space.

As the countdown to lift-off continued, the action on the Orbiter's flight deck increased, though each move was carefully double-checked by other crew members. On the last Apollo mission, the joint American–Russian spaceflight, one of the crew failed to turn on two switches during the descent, with the result that poisonous gases leaked into the capsule. The crew had been lucky to escape with their lives, but the mistake had brought home to other crews the lesson that no matter how routine spaceflights might become, errors could still be fatal.

The countdown, using an automatic system based on a computer, took only 2 to 3 hours for the Shuttle, compared with more than a day for Apollo. Towards the end of the countdown the service tower swung away. This contained the escape slides which the crew could use if any emergency arose before take-off. If anything went wrong after the take-off, the Orbiter could either return to the launch site after climbing to 110,000 metres or complete one orbit before landing. Stewart and Greene had spent about 600 hours in a simulator preparing for just such an emergency.

Into orbit

Three seconds before lift-off, Stewart ignited the three main engines at the base of the Orbiter as it stood vertical on the pad. With one second to go, the two solid rocket boosters lit up and the Shuttle assembly, weighing 2,000 tonnes, rose vertically, accelerating gradually until after 2 minutes it was travelling at 5,000 kph. At that point, the boosters were jettisoned and fell back on parachutes into the Atlantic, where they were recovered and returned to Kennedy to be used again. After 8 minutes, the engines had used all the fuel in the massive external tank, and normally the tank was separated and burned up as it re-entered the atmosphere. On this mission, however, the tank was to be used in the construction of a permanent space station so Stewart ignited the motors of the onboard manoeuvring

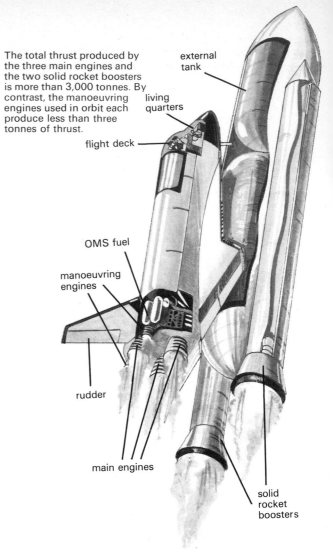

The total thrust produced by the three main engines and the two solid rocket boosters is more than 3,000 tonnes. By contrast, the manoeuvring engines used in orbit each produce less than three tonnes of thrust.

external tank

living quarters

flight deck

OMS fuel

manoeuvring engines

rudder

main engines

solid rocket boosters

system (OMS) on the Orbiter, and both the tank and the Orbiter settled into a steady orbit.

On the flight deck, Stewart and Greene moved their seats from the horizontal take-off position, though now the craft and its crew were weightless so that *up* and *down* held little meaning. Greene had completed an underwater 'Zero-G' (zero gravity) course during his astronaut training, but he was still unprepared for the curious sensations created by standing on his head on what used to be called the ceiling. The spacecraft was, of course, designed for such conditions, and had straps fitted where the crew could tie themselves down, especially when sleeping. Even the washing and toilet facilities were specially designed to cope with weightlessness.

The first task was to open the cargo doors as the insides of the doors acted as radiators to let out the unwanted heat from the *Discovery*. Once opened, these exposed the pallets on which were mounted the Spacelab experiments. As the scientists got to work, Stewart and Greene were manoeuvring the spacecraft into the same orbit as the space station which was being built from parts brought up by the Shuttle. Once they were alongside, Gordon Fulwell, who was responsible for the in-orbit operation of *Discovery*, used the 15-metre-long remote manipulating arm to place the external tank in position as part of the space station's structure. The arm was operated by a control column and had a television camera mounted above the 'hand' to give a picture on a screen in *Discovery*'s cabin. The arm could only exert a few kilograms pressure, not enough to lift a box of groceries on Earth, but in the weightlessness of space, it located the 40-tonne external tank precisely in its place. It would then be converted into living accommodation for the scientists based on the station.

Tasks and experiments

Once relieved of the fuel tank, Stewart again used the OMS, which had its own fuel supply, to take the Orbiter down to a lower orbit. A large-frame camera on board could then continue the task of photographing all the Earth's surface, a task which had been started on previous Shuttle flights. Taken from a height of 250 kilometres these photographs could detect objects as small as 11 square metres, which meant that even small buildings would show up. From the film brought back to Earth, very detailed maps of the whole Earth's surface could be composed.

The Shuttle can be used to recover spacecraft from orbit and return them to Earth instead of them burning up when they re-enter the atmosphere.

Once the scientists and specialists had settled to their tasks, Glen Stewart had some time to relax. He was constantly amazed by the amount of living space available in the Shuttle. The Orbiters were limited to about one week in space, though the latest Orbiters, *Discovery* and her sister *Atlantis*, could carry a large solar array which generated more electrical power and enabled the Orbiters to stay in orbit for longer periods. Despite the short time spent in space, the living area was much more comfortable than in earlier spacecraft, especially than that in the Gemini Glen had first flown.

The Gemini had carried 2 men and weighed just 3·5 tonnes, while the Orbiter could carry 7 men, including 4 scientists, and weighed 114 tonnes. All the crew facilities on the Orbiter, including rest and toilet areas, were on a separate level below the flight deck, and this area also accommodated 3 of the scientists during launch and re-entry. On some of the Spacelab flights a pressurized module was carried on one of the pallets in the cargo bay. This provided a working area for the scientists who occupied it for 12-hour shifts while carrying out their experiments. On this flight one of the experiments, which was disliked by Glen and his co-pilot, was called 'the Sled'. It required one of the astronauts to act as a guineapig by sitting on a chair which was propelled along rails set in the floor. The astronaut could be turned in the chair to face in various directions, while being subject to a gentle acceleration. Due to the weightless conditions on

the spacecraft, such movement could make the guineapig feel dizzy and quite ill. This was a common problem, but through this research, the scientists hoped to find a cure.

A problem
Although all possible precautions were taken during space flights, problems did occasionally crop up. The worst was on Apollo 13 when a fuel tank burst and an immediate return to Earth was required. The only way this could be done was to use the Moon's gravitational pull to swing the spacecraft round to a safe landing back on Earth.

On *Discovery* the only problem which appeared was of a less dramatic nature, but was nevertheless potentially dangerous. The cargo doors refused to shut. While this presented no immediate difficulties, the stresses caused by re-entry could easily tear off the 18-metre long doors, and damage the Orbiter, unless they were locked shut. The only answer was for someone to leave the Orbiter and shut them manually from the outside.

Stewart and Gordon Fulwell donned their spacesuits in the *Discovery*'s living quarters. These suits were specially designed for Shuttle operations and were rather different from the suits Stewart and Fulwell had worn on the Apollo missions. No longer did each astronaut have his personal suit specially made to measure. Instead, a selection of parts – arms, torso and legs – was chosen from five standard fittings. There were no zips as all connections were by stainless steel clips, and the joints incorporated roller bearings to make movement easier. The boots were permanently attached to the legs of the suit. Underneath, the astronauts wore a set of liquid-cooled underwear which circulated a cooling liquid from the life-support system carried on their backs. This unit also housed the oxygen system, and a

The manoeuvring pack worn during extra-vehicular activity propels the astronaut around the outside of the spacecraft and is so reliable that there is no safety line between the astronaut and his ship.

Trips outside the Orbiter, or space-walks, should only be necessary to make emergency repairs to the spacecraft.

Below: The flight deck of the Orbiter bears some resemblance to that of commercial airliners.

manoeuvring pack which used small rockets. The whole suit was topped by a helmet incorporating a visor to reduce the glare of the sun.

Thus equipped, Stewart and Fulwell climbed through the airlock to the outside of *Discovery*. They did not need to attach safety lines as they wore manoeuvring packs. These were used to propel them where they wanted in space. The astronauts quickly made their way back to the jammed cargo door, where they expected to crank the door shut by hand. They kept in touch with each other and with Houston Control at the Johnson Space Centre by using the radio units built into the life-support packs. While Stewart was examining one side of *Discovery* he heard Fulwell's voice calling him to the rear of the cargo bay. When he got there he found that some of the thermal insulation tiles had come loose and were jamming the doors. While the mission specialist cleared the tiles out of the way, Stewart returned to the *Discovery* to collect a repair kit for the tiles. This was one of the problems which the amazing pre-planning by the Shuttle team had provided for. Within an hour the doors were shut, and the *Discovery* was ready for re-entry.

Return to Earth

For the first part of its return to Earth *Discovery* behaved as any other spacecraft. Its manoeuvring engines were used to leave orbit and to brake its descent until it entered the atmosphere, travelling at 280,000 kph. As it descended, it behaved more like an aeroplane. At 12,000 metres, Stewart took normal control, using the control column for pitch and roll control. The throttle, which was previously linked to the main engines, was now connected to the large airbrake at the tail to vary the rate of descent.

Normally, returning Orbiters carried out an automatic landing on the specially built 4·75-kilometre-long runway at Kennedy Space Centre, but as this was his last trip Stewart exercised his discretion and decided to make a manual landing. Fifteen kilometres from touchdown, he slowed to subsonic speeds, and turned on to a heading given to him by the approach controller to intercept the runway's microwave landing system which guided him over the last few kilometres. Flying without power and at high speed, the *Discovery* descended very steeply towards the touchdown point. Three kilometres from the runway the descent angle was 25° compared with the 3° glide slope followed by airliners. At about 300 metres Stewart began to flare *Discovery*, which meant that he raised the nose and allowed the speed to reduce towards the optimum touchdown speed of 350 kph. With a slight thump, *Discovery* landed and drew to a halt at the end of Kennedy's main runway, only a short distance from the launch pad it had left six days earlier.

1. The main engines and solid rocket boosters ignite and lift the Shuttle vertically from the launch pad at Kennedy Space Centre.

2. At 50 kilometres high, the solid rocket boosters burn out, separate from the spacecraft, and return to Earth on parachutes. They are recovered and used again.

3. Travelling at more than 25,000 kph, the main engines are shut down before the Orbiter reaches the speed at which it orbits the earth.

4. The external tank is separated, unless it is to be used for satellite construction, and it burns up as it passes through the atmosphere.

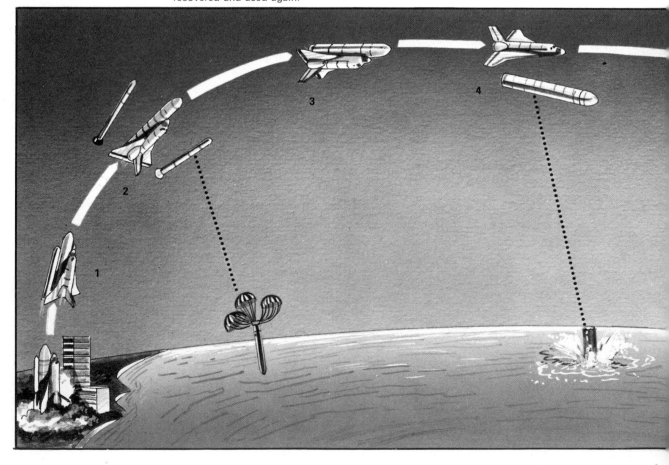

Above: Thermal tiles insulate the spacecraft from the high temperatures experienced in re-entry.

Within three weeks, *Discovery* would be back on the launch pad ready for another mission. Stewart, however, had made his contribution to man's knowledge of the space surrounding him, and he retired to a desk job in Washington. In some ways he was glad to have finished, for the further exploration of space was now a job for the scientists.

5. A short burn by the OMS engines places the Orbiter in orbit. Once the mission is completed, the spacecraft is turned round and the engines fire to slow it down.

6. The Orbiter descends through the atmosphere and down to the runway like a glider. Touchdown is at 350 kph, and the runway is 4·75 kilometres long.

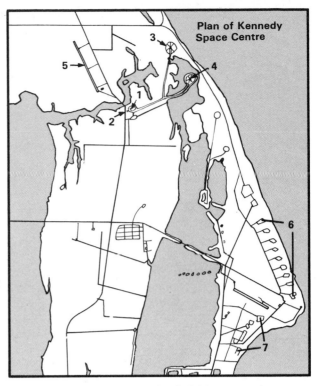

Plan of Kennedy Space Centre

Key: 1. Vehicle assembly building 2. Orbiter processing building 3. and 4. Shuttle launch pads 5. Orbiter runway 6. and 7. Other launch pads

Below: Rocket launches have grown in size to the massive Saturn V, used to send the Apollo spacecraft to the Moon. The Shuttle is small in comparison.

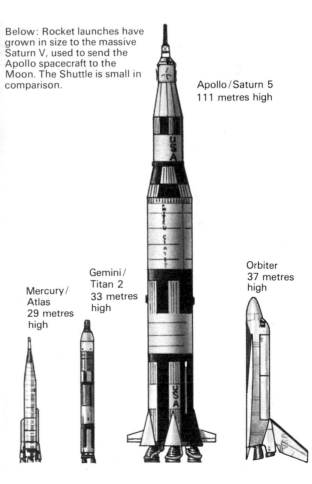

Apollo/Saturn 5
111 metres high

Mercury/Atlas
29 metres high

Gemini/Titan 2
33 metres high

Orbiter
37 metres high

Index